Stockwin's
MARITIME
Miscellany

'But this learned I from my dear mother –
The kiss of a seaman's worth two of another'
– Anon, *Roxburghe Ballads,* seventeenth century

Stockwin's MARITIME *Miscellany*

❋

A DITTY BAG OF WONDERS
from the
GOLDEN AGE OF SAIL

Julian Stockwin

EBURY
PRESS

5 7 9 10 8 6 4

Published in 2009 by Ebury Press, an imprint of Ebury Publishing

A Random House Group Company

Copyright © Julian Stockwin 2009

Julian Stockwin has asserted his right to be identified as the author of this
Work in accordance with the Copyright, Designs and Patents Act 1988

The Random House Group Limited Reg. No. 954009

Addresses for companies within the Random House Group can be found at
www.randomhouse.co.uk

A CIP catalogue record for this book is available from the British Library

The Random House Group Limited supports The Forest Stewardship
Council (FSC®), the leading international forest certification organisation.
Our books carrying the FSC label are printed on FSC® certified paper.
FSC is the only forest certification scheme endorsed by the leading
environmental organisations, including Greenpeace.
Our paper procurement policy can be found at
www.randomhouse.co.uk/environment

To buy books by your favourite authors and register for offers visit
www.randomhouse.co.uk

Typeset by Palimpsest Book Production Limited,
Falkirk, Stirlingshire
Printed and bound in Great Britain by Clays Ltd, St Ives plc

ISBN 9780091930660

Contents

Foreword

I've no idea where my love of Neptune's Realm comes from, but it's been a part of me from as far back as I can remember. My mother tells of a very small boy once bringing home a dead sea-bird because it stank so richly of the sea. While none of my immediate family had any salty connections there *was* a distant relative, Tom Clay, who had sailed around the Horn in the lovely clipper *Cutty Sark*, and his stirring tales of iron men in wooden ships could only strengthen my determination to become a sailor. At school I was a dismal scholar, all the time daydreaming of sailing over the horizon to some foreign shore. My father hoped to knock this nonsense out of me by sending me to a tough sea-training school at the age of 14, but it didn't work and I joined the navy as soon as I could. I had adventures around the world and served both on the lower deck and later as an officer. After swallowing the anchor it's such a joy to have come full circle and earn my living now by writing about the sea, which I've done for the past ten years.

When I was approached by Ebury Press I jumped at the challenge of compiling a selection of maritime wonders from the days of sail. Before steam came along man still had to *woo* the sea, utterly dependent on the wind and the currents – and his nautical skills. The great historical sweep of five centuries that began with the heroic voyages of discovery in the fifteenth century and culminated in the glorious reign of the clipper ship in the 1860s is truly the Golden Age of Sail.

I wish you Fair Winds!

JULIAN STOCKWIN
2009

Chapter 1.

Nautical
FACTS & FEATS

Nautical
FACTS & FEATS

Introduction

The Golden Age of Sail is the mother lode for history's most colourful people and amazing incidents. Where else could you find characters like English seaman turned samurai Richard Adams, who did much to open up Japan to the West in the early seventeenth century; Admiral Richard ('Black Dick') Howe of the Royal Navy, who was said never to smile unless a battle was about to begin, and the Russian tsar who loved to disguise himself as a common shipwright and work in an English dockyard? Yet the fairer sex could sometimes demonstrate just as much courage and determination as their men at sea. The last invasion of Britain was not in 1066 at Hastings but in 1797 at a little town in southwest Wales, where troops who had been landed from four French warships surrendered because of the feisty local women.

One of the notable characteristics of this era was sheer bloody-mindedness in the face of incredible odds. When Sir Richard Grenville chose to stand and fight the Spanish in 1591 he was outgunned and outnumbered 53 to one. William Bligh achieved one of the most remarkable feats of seaman-ship and survival of all time: after mutineers set him adrift in an open boat, he completed an epic voyage across the Pacific Ocean without the loss of a single man. At the Battle of Trafalgar the diminutive French captain Jean

Lucas and his crew fought heroically in *Redoutable* as their decks were torn open and guns shattered. When he eventually surrendered just one mast remained upright. The butcher's bill was horrendous – 88 per cent of the crew were either killed or injured.

It was an age when a barren rock could be commissioned as a sloop of war, when a duel to the death could be fought by a naval officer over a dog, and when the French could say of the English that they felt it wise to execute an admiral from time to time *pour encourager les autres*. And who could not smile today at the gritty humour of the handsome Irish master's mate Jack Spratt? When told that his badly mangled leg must be amputated he refused and pointing to his good leg declared, 'Where shall I find a match for this?'

Facing almost certain death at sea, William Bligh is cast adrift by Bounty *mutineers.*

THE WAR OF JENKINS'S EAR

It may be history's most oddly named conflict. Captain Robert Jenkins was an English sea captain whose ship *Rebecca* was boarded by the Spanish as he sailed back to England from Jamaica in 1731. During the ensuing skirmish one of Jenkins's ears was severed and he pickled it in a bottle. Although he complained of his treatment on his return, that was pretty much that for another seven years.

Friction had been increasing between the English and Spanish over trade rights in Central America, and in 1738 Jenkins was summoned to Parliament to recount his story and produce the now shrivelled body part. This resulted in outrage throughout the country but more importantly it was an excuse to teach the Spanish a lesson. England declared war on Spain the following year – and thus began the War of Jenkins's Ear.

Admiral Vernon was ordered to 'destroy the Spanish settlements in the West Indies and distress their shipping by every method whatever'. He took the city of Porto Bello in November 1739, a victory that was greeted with much celebration in England, giving rise to a number of commemorative names including Portobello Road in London.

Vernon took Porto Bello with just six ships.

'*N*EVER A STRUGGLE MORE MARVELLOUS OR MORE CLOSELY CONTESTED'

In the nineteenth century a sailing ship of great beauty, grace and speed evolved – the clipper. Carrying a very large spread of sails on three or more masts, these were the greyhounds of the sea and ideally suited for high-value, low-bulk cargoes such as China tea. They achieved record-breaking sailing times, often in spectacular races with other clippers to be the first to land their cargo.

The Great Tea Race of 1866 was a nail-biting event from start to finish. In the spring nine clippers assembled at the Pagoda Anchorage of the Min River at Foochow, jostling to take on board the new season tea as quickly as possible. The first vessel to unload the precious cargo in London could claim an extra ten shillings a ton in freight charges. Huge sums of money were bet on the outcome of the race, and English tea merchants in Mincing Lane were ready to begin bidding the moment they tasted samples of the sought-after first tea of the season from the fastest clipper.

Its 24,000-km route took the ships across the South China Sea, through the Sunda Strait of Indonesia, across the Indian Ocean, round the Cape of Good Hope and up the Atlantic Ocean to the English Channel. The five leading vessels were often in sight of each other, passing and repassing as they knifed through the waves.

The race generated great excitement as the fastest vessels entered British waters virtually neck and neck. The *Daily Telegraph* of 12 September reported: 'A struggle more closely contested or more marvellous... has probably never before been witnessed. *Taeping*... arrived at the Lizard in the same hour as *Ariel*, her nearest rival, and then dashed up the Channel, the two ships abreast of each other. During the entire day they gallantly ran side by side, carried on by a strong westerly wind, every stitch of canvas set, and the sea sweeping their decks as they careered before the gale.'

Taeping, carrying 695 metric tons of tea, won the race by a whisker, taking 99 days to sail to London and docking just half an hour ahead of *Ariel*. In the spirit of sportsmanship the two ships' owners split the winner's premium.

Taeping *and* Ariel.

AT CLOSE QUARTERS – at close range.

DERIVATION: in the seventeenth century hand-to-hand fights when ships were boarded by the enemy were known as 'close-fight' engagements, and the term was also applied to the barriers the sailors erected to keep assailants at bay. By the mid-eighteenth century this confined defensive space had come to be known as 'close quarters'.

*I*T'S NOT A ROCK, IT'S A SHIP!

In January 1804 the Royal Navy took possession of a rock, 180 m high, 1.6 km off Martinique, the centre of French power in the Caribbean – and then declared the barren pinnacle a warship. This uninhabited islet was an ideal site for establishing a blockade as it dominated the approach to Port Royal, the capital of Martinique. And, with a visibility of 64 km from the summit, a signal station could be set up to pass on intelligence about French ship movements.

However, there were a large number of obstacles to be overcome. The only landing spot was on the western side; heavy swells and narrow rock ledges made any attempt to do so very chancy; and there was no food or water on the island.

Commodore Samuel Hood had reconnoitred the rock in his flagship HMS *Centaur* and was well aware of the challenges it posed. Fortunately his first lieutenant, James Maurice, was an amateur mountaineer and he went ashore and found a route up the sheer rock face.

A working party with several weeks' provisions was landed. They found dry caves where they set up operations. With the aid of pitons and ropes the nimble seamen, used to swarming up rigging, scaled the heights and installed rope ladders. One hazard they had not bargained on, however, was the deadly local snake, the *fer-de-lance*.

Eventually the defences of Diamond Rock comprised two 24-pounders just above sea level, a 24-pounder halfway up and two 18-pounder cannon right on top. Getting these massive weapons in place was a heroic undertaking which took long backbreaking days at the capstan. After a line was run ashore a cable was rigged from the mainmast of the anchored *Centaur* to the top of the cliff, and the big guns were painstakingly hauled to the rock using an ingenious sling. Then began the formidable task of landing water and provisions for 120 men.

Maurice was installed ashore as commander, and in front of the assembled sailors and marines he proudly read out his commission. A pennant was run up and Diamond Rock was officially rated a sloop of war.

An artist, John Eckstein, obtained Hood's permission to record for posterity one of the most outstanding achievements of the age of sail. He painted a series of aquatints which were published in 1805. Eckstein was amazed at the ingenuity of Jack Tar and said, 'I shall never more take my hat off for anything less than a British seaman.'

For a year and a half the British fired at any passing French ship and proved such a thorn in the side of Admiral Villeneuve on his way to his destiny at Trafalgar that he eventually threw his entire battle fleet at the rock. On 2 June 1805 Captain James Maurice surrendered. It was not French firepower that defeated him, however, but an earth tremor which cracked the water cistern he had installed.

In the Royal Navy, there was (and is to this day) an automatic court of enquiry if a captain lost his ship, whatever the reason. This rule applied even if the ship was a rock, so a court was convened aboard HMS *Circe* on 24 June. It did not take long to reach the verdict that Maurice and his officers had done everything in their power to the very last in the defence of the rock and against a most superior force.

'*T*HE SEA WOLF'

Thomas Cochrane was one of the most daring and successful captains of the Napoleonic wars, called '*le loup des mers*', the sea wolf, by Napoleon Bonaparte. In the course of his career he captured 50 enemy ships in just one year, was dismissed from the Royal Navy for alleged fraud, commanded the navies of Chile, Brazil and Greece, and was eventually reinstated in the Royal Navy as an admiral. He was a radical politician, an early advocate of many technological innovations that were later adopted by the navy and the inspiration for a number of fiction writers.

But in many ways Cochrane was his own worst enemy and made several powerful foes, especially in his political campaign against corruption in the navy. Earl St Vincent, although sympathetic to some of Cochrane's beliefs, said of him that he was 'mad, romantic, money-getting and not truth telling'.

One of Cochrane's most famous exploits occurred on 6 May 1801 when he took the 32-gun Spanish frigate *El Gamo* and its crew of 300. His vessel, the 14-gun brig-sloop HMS *Speedy*, had a crew of just 50. On spotting *El Gamo* Cochrane hoisted the Stars and Stripes (whose country Spain was not at war with) and sailed directly towards her. When he drew close he lowered this flag, hoisted the Union Jack and began firing. His first salvo killed the Spanish captain. Cochrane stormed the ship with a boarding party which included his entire crew, except the ship's surgeon who was left in charge of the wheel. A ferocious fight with cutlasses, axes and pikes ensued. At one point Cochrane called loudly for another 50 (fictitious) reinforcements to follow – and the Spanish surrendered.

But the plucky little ship's luck did not last and *Speedy* was later taken by the French, who gave her to the Pope renamed *San Paulo*.

Personally bold and adventurous, Cochrane nevertheless took great pains to ensure the safety of his men and was greatly admired by them. To his ship's company he was a second Nelson and they were intensely loyal to him.

Saving The Dog

Cochrane once risked his life for a dog. Having lit the fuse on a fireship packed with explosives he was being rowed away when he remembered the ship's pet was still aboard. He hastily turned the boat back and rescued the dog. Ironically, had he not been delayed by the rescue his boat would have been directly under the falling wreckage and all aboard probably killed. As it happened, the deadly debris flew right over the top of them.

Cochrane's kindness could extend to the enemy. In command of the frigate HMS *Pallas* he captured the Spanish ship *La Fortuna* laden with gold and silver and valuable merchandise. Troubled when he heard of the hardship that would be caused to the Spanish captain and his merchant passenger in losing their entire private fortune that was aboard the vessel, Cochrane gained the agreement of his officers and seamen that the two Spaniards should be given 5,000 Spanish dollars each so that they and their families would not be ruined.

Thomas Cochrane,
10th Earl of
Dundonald.

Not a mark on him

As the ship was about to engage the enemy, Captain Thomas Hardy's clerk Thomas Whipple was checking some details with a midshipman on the deck of HMS *Victory* when a cannonball slammed by. Whipple dropped dead instantly without even a bruise on his body, but his companion remained completely unhurt. This phenomenon had a variety of names – 'wind of ball', 'wind of the shot', *'vent du boulet'* and 'breath of the cannon ball'. It is a form of blast injury caused by a rapid change in pressure, particularly in air-containing organs of the body. One naval surgeon in Nelson's time described it as a 'peculiar accident... common in engagements at sea', and went on to explain:

If a cannon ball in its flight passes close to any part of the body, that part is rendered livid and benumbed for some time. It is most dangerous when it approaches the stomach and has often in such cases proved instantaneously fatal without the least mark of injury. At other times marks of violence are conspicuous. What is remarkable is this, that the wind of a ball had never been fatal on the head.

JURY RIG – something assembled in a makeshift manner.
DERIVATION: in sailing ships it was sometimes necessary to improvise a temporary replacement for an item such as a damaged mast or a disabled rudder and thus enable the vessel to keep going until the nearest port could be made and the stop-gap replaced. The origin of 'jury' is not known, but it has been suggested that sailors coined it as a shortened form of 'injury-rigged'.

A SHIP THAT LIVED UP TO HER NAME

In command of the rickety old galleon *Revenge* Sir Richard Grenville was separated from the rest of the English fleet off the Azores in 1591.

He could have fled but he chose to stand and fight the Spanish, outgunned and outnumbered 53 to one. Despite these insane odds *Revenge* battled all through the night and the next day and, beating off all attempts to board her, destroyed two Spanish ships. At one stage Grenville ordered his own ship to be sunk, rather than see her go to the enemy, but then relented on condition that the Spanish spare the lives of his crew. Grenville, who had been gravely wounded, died aboard the Spanish flagship several days later.

Revenge lived up to her name – less than a week after the battle, with a 200-man Spanish prize crew aboard, she was lost with all hands in a vicious storm. The ship's valiant deeds have ensured that she is one of the most renowned in naval history, and a number of ships have proudly borne her name, including one at the Battle of Trafalgar. The most recent *Revenge* was a Polaris submarine launched in 1969 and retired several years ago.

Tennyson celebrated Grenville's bravery in his poem 'The Revenge: a Ballad of the Fleet', which includes this exhortation from Grenville:

'At sea or ashore
We die – does it matter when?
Sink me the ship, Master Gunner – sink her, split her in twain!
Fall into the hands of God, not into the hands of Spain!'

Early nineteenth-century print depicting the last hours of Revenge's *heroic fight.*

THE MAN IN THE LODGE

Portsmouth Historic Dockyard's oldest surviving building is the Porter's Lodge, built in 1708. Ellis Markant was its first occupant and lived there until his death. He was the public face of the dockyard, the daily interface between the inside and outside communities. One of his most important duties concerned the dockyard muster bell; if it didn't ring the town wouldn't wake, shops wouldn't open and men wouldn't get to work on time.

His job was 'to be constantly attending at the gate to open and shut the same for all comers and goers into and out...' He had to guard the dock-yard and its contents, allowing 'no person to pass out of the dock gates with great coats, large trousers or any other outer dress that can conceal stores of any kind'.

There were some perks to the job; Markant could sell small beer in the summertime, 'such as is fit to quench the parties thirst that drinks thereof, and to enable them to better to perform their labour, and not such as will distemper them'. His garden produced medicinal herbs such as feverfew (for headache) and thyme (used as a tonic) as well as vegetables for the ships.

AT LOGGERHEADS – in a state of serious disagreement, a sort of metaphysical butting of heads!

DERIVATION: a loggerhead was an implement used aboard ship in caulking the seams in deck timbers. It consisted of a hollow iron sphere at the end of a shaft. The sphere was heated in a fire and then plunged into a bucket of pitch. This melted the pitch, which was then applied to the seams. A hot loggerhead was definitely something to keep away from...

*T*RAITOR TYRIE

 The last time a hanging, drawing and quartering punishment took place in Britain was on 24 August 1782, at Portsmouth. Scottish spy David Tyrie had been convicted for carrying on a treasonable correspondence with the French. A contemporary account records that he was hanged for 22 minutes and then his head was cut off and his heart cut out and burned. He was then emasculated and quartered, his body parts put in a coffin and buried in the pebbles at the seaside. Immediately after the burial sailors dug up the coffin and cut the body into pieces as souvenirs.

*S*TOP THE CARRIAGE!

 On 26 January 1796 Captain Edward Pellew of the frigate HMS *Indefatigable,* dressed in splendid full dress uniform, and accompanied by his wife, was on his way to a formal dinner in Plymouth, a thriving port town near one of the Royal Navy's most important naval bases. Their route took them past the open space above the sea cliffs known as the Hoe, with its magnificent view over the harbour – where Francis Drake had famously played bowls in the face of invasion by the Spanish Armada.

Despite stormy weather crowds were gathered on the Hoe gesturing excitedly out to sea. Pellew stopped his carriage and went to investigate.

It soon became clear that *Dutton*, a troopship bound for the West Indies, had run on to rocks. Lying broadside against smashing waves she had lost her masts and was listing badly; the imminent loss of all aboard seemed in no doubt.

Pellew urged the onlookers to help (including the officers of *Dutton*, who enraged Pellew at having abandoned the passengers to their fate) – but nobody was willing to risk his life in the seething waters. The situation was desperate, so Pellew decided to go it alone. Quickly discarding his fine attire he threw himself into the sea and seizing the hawser (a large ship's rope) that the officers had used to save themselves, and which was still attached to the ship, hauled himself hand over hand out to the stricken vessel. On the way timbers from the wrecked masts slammed into his back, but he ignored the pain. When he reached *Dutton* he clambered on deck and drew his sword. Assuming command, he told the frightened passengers three things: that they would all be saved if they quietly obeyed his orders, that he would be the last to quit the wreck – and that he would run through anyone who disobeyed him.

Order was swiftly brought to the chaos aboard, despite the fact that many of the soldiers, believing their end was near, had resorted to drink and were in a sorry state of inebriation. Pellew managed to get two additional hawsers ashore and contrived an ingenious endless rope cradle to convey passengers to safety. Others were taken off in boats that rescuers had eventually managed to bring alongside.

All of the some 500 men, women and children aboard were saved, including a three-week-old baby. Shortly after Pellew left, *Dutton* broke up and sank.

Pellew served the Royal Navy with great distinction for 50 years. He was undoubtedly one of the greatest fighting captains of the Napoleonic wars but has been somewhat overshadowed by Horatio Nelson. He died in 1833, a vice-admiral of the United Kingdom, peer of the realm and holder of many foreign honours.

$\mathcal{A}$ GLASS OF PUNCH, SIR?

The Right Honourable Edward Russel was captain-general and commander-in-chief of His Majesty's forces in the Mediterranean. On 25 October 1694 he served a rather special punch from a marble fountain in his garden at Alicante, Spain. The ingredients of the beverage were

4 hogsheads of brandy, 8 hogsheads of water, 25,000 lemons, 75 l of lime juice, 560 kg of fine white Lisbon sugar, 3 kg of grated nutmeg, 300 toasted biscuits and a pipe of dry mountain Malaga. Russel had a large canopy constructed to keep off the rain, and a ship's boy rowed around the fountain in a mahogany boat, filling the cups of the 6,000 assembled guests. When the poor lad became overcome with the fumes, another took his place.

CUTS NO ICE – makes little or no impression.
DERIVATION: from an ineffective vessel that could not make much progress in the autumn pack ice of the Baltic.

Windsor Castle Wins the Day

At dawn on 1 October 1807 off Guadeloupe in the Caribbean, the lookout in *Windsor Castle* saw enemy sail rapidly overhauling them and the ship prepared to defend itself. With no prospect of escape the 28-man crew rigged the anti-boarding nets and went to quarters. The French privateer *Jeune Richard,* its crew of 92 outnumbering that of the *Windsor Castle* by more than three to one and with close to double their weight of metal, quickly closed in, but the nets prevented them from boarding.

Acting-Captain William Rogers prepared *Windsor Castle* for action and stood by to sink the ship should it be necessary to keep her out of enemy hands. After a fierce close-in fight over several hours in which *Jeune Richard* was severely damaged Rogers and just five men then stormed aboard the French vessel, killing the captain and tearing down their colours. Losses on the British side were 3 killed, 10 wounded; the French suffered 21 dead and 33 wounded.

Given the odds, this was a remarkable victory in itself, but *Windsor Castle* was no naval warship but a civilian vessel, a lightly armed Falmouth packet, run by the Post Office to carry mail, freight and passengers overseas.

The news of how Rogers had turned upon his pursuer and taken her as a prize caused a sensation in England. Among the many rewards Rogers received was the full captaincy of another packet ship.

NEW MEANING TO 'MIND OVER MATTER'

Lord Horatio Nelson has been voted England's greatest hero, the man who led the nation to her most glorious victories at sea.

Yet this revered figure suffered so much throughout his life from disease and injury that he brings special meaning to the phrase 'mind over matter'. He was wounded more times than any other Royal Navy admiral during the Napoleonic Wars. Ironically, Copenhagen, the hardest fought of all his battles, was the only one in which he was not hurt.

In his teens, serving in India, the young Horatio became ill with the first of many fevers that would turn his hair prematurely grey before the age of 25.

In July 1794, while engaged in the siege of Calvi in Corsica, he received his first serious battle wound and subsequently lost the use of his right eye. During the Battle of St Vincent in 1797 he suffered an internal trauma, and abdominal pain troubled him greatly in later years.

At Tenerife, in the Canary Islands, on the night of 24 July that same year he was leading a desperate assault ashore when he was struck in the upper right arm by a musket-ball. A tourniquet fashioned by his stepson saved his life. It is typical of Nelson that he refused to go back aboard his own ship HMS *Seahorse* in case he alarmed Betsy Fremantle, the wife of the captain, who was at sea with her husband at the time. Instead he was rowed to HMS *Theseus*, where his right arm was amputated. (Later, recalling the shock of the cold steel of the surgeon's knife, he included in his fleet orders the instruction that henceforth all such instruments be warmed before use.)

At the Battle of the Nile Nelson sustained a wound to his forehead which cut right to the bone; the flesh fell over his good eye, temporarily blinding him.

Finally, at Trafalgar, a ball from an enemy musket struck the epaulette on his left shoulder and penetrated through his lung to the spine – where some of the gold braid from his epaulette was found to be still adhering to it. Nelson was carried below to the orlop deck in great pain; he died at 4.30 p.m., after stoically enduring for another two hours 45 minutes.

A French sniper mortally wounds Nelson. Today, a small brass plaque marks the spot he fell on Victory's *quarterdeck.*

WOMEN IN RED

The annals of history record the name of Hastings as the site of the last invasion of Britain. But there is another contender – the town of Fishguard in southwest Wales. And the story of this attempt by France's revolutionary government to liberate England is proof positive that the women ashore in the age of sail had just as much spunk as their men at sea!

On 22 February 1797 the French set in motion a plan to divert British troops away from Ireland so they could launch a major attack there. Some 1,400 soldiers led by Colonel William Tate, an American, were landed from four French warships on the shore of Carreg Wastad, just west of Fishguard.

However, the French were to have only two days on British soil. At the sight of military reinforcements mustering on the nearby hills they surrendered to the local militia led by Lord Cawdor. In fact it was not British Army Redcoats they saw, but hundreds of Welsh women in their traditional scarlet cloaks. One local woman is particularly celebrated as the heroine of the hour – Jemima Nicholas, a 47-year-old Fishguard cobbler, who advanced on 12 Frenchmen with a pitchfork and captured them all single-handedly.

A magnificent record of the event, 'The Last Invasion Tapestry', over 30 m long and in the style of the Bayeux Tapestry, is now on display at the Fishguard Town Hall.

>   A WEATHER EYE – alertness for a sudden change in
> the situation. DERIVATION: in the open sea the lookout
> watched on the weather, or windward, side of the ship. The first
> sign of a change always came on this side.

$\mathcal{B}$URIED TWICE

During the Battle of Trafalgar 21-year-old Lieutenant William Ram on board HMS *Victory* was badly wounded by vicious wooden shards splintering out with the impact of round shot from *Redoutable*. Bleeding severely, Ram was carried below to the cockpit, where the surgeon did what he could to staunch the haemorrhage. When told of the severity of his injuries, Ram was so distraught that he tore off the ligatures that were being applied and rapidly bled to death. Along with other casualties he was committed to the deep.

Several days later his body was washed up on the Spanish coast and found by some English prisoners of war who identified the corpse from Ram's name stitched into his shirt. They obtained permission from the governor of Cadiz to give him a Christian burial.

$\mathcal{S}$COURGE OF THE SLAVERS

  The Royal Navy played a vital but little-known role in suppressing slavery. After the evil trade was outlawed by the British Parliament in 1807 the West Africa Squadron was established the following year. Initially the unit was limited to intercepting British slave ships, fining them £100 for every slave found aboard, but it expanded to target slavers from other countries.

The West Africa Squadron patrolled the 5,000 km of the West African coast for 60 years and at its height accounted for one-sixth of the resources of the Royal Navy and Royal Marines. The squadron seized 1,600 vessels and liberated 150,000 slaves, and played as important a role as the campaigners led by William Wilberforce in bringing slavery to an end.

One of the most successful ships was poacher-turned-gamekeeper HMS *Black Joke*. A captured slave ship, she had originally sailed under the name of *Henrietta*. With a fair wind *Black Joke* was capable of overhauling the best on the coast and although only lightly armed she quickly became the scourge of the slavers.

Among *Black Joke*'s most notable conquests was the Spanish brig *El Almirante*. The slaver was sighted on 1 February 1829 and although her quarry was vastly superior in size and arms *Black Joke* immediately gave chase. The winds were light and variable and *Black Joke* had to resort to sweeps to close the gap. The chase lasted 11 hours under the blazing sun and the light was fading as a desperate duel began. When the Spanish vessel finally surrendered it had 15 crew dead and 13 wounded. *Black Joke* had suffered six wounded, two of whom later died. Over 450 slaves were found chained together in appalling conditions in the hold of *El Almirante*.

In one year alone *Black Joke* took 22 ships and liberated 7,000 slaves. Sometimes she worked in tandem with another ship. In September 1831 she was sailing with the schooner HMS *Fair Rosamond* off the mouth of the Bonny River when they surprised two Spanish slavers. Recognising the Royal Navy ships the vessels fled back up the river and *Black Joke* and *Fair Rosamond* gave chase. As they were overhauled the Spanish began throwing slaves over the side. Some were chained together in pairs and quickly drowned. Others tried to make for the shore but were attacked by sharks and torn to pieces. The four vessels crammed on all sail as they raced up the river. Eventually the slavers were captured and what remained of their sorry human cargo given their freedom.

HMS *Black Joke* met an inglorious end in May 1832. Her timbers rotten, she was condemned by Admiralty surveyors and burnt. All that remains of her is an envelope filled with brown dust in the Public Record Office at Kew in southwest London.

There was a huge human cost for the men who served in the West Africa Squadron. Much of daily life was tedious and there was little chance of promotion as a result of a celebrated victory in a famous battle. Fever was rife and between 1830 and 1865 some 1,600 men in the West Africa Squadron died. In one year about 25 per cent of the officers and men died, a proportion 15 times higher than the navy had ever lost in wartime in any year.

Speedy topsail schooners were favoured by slave traders on the west coast of Africa.

FINEST SINGLE-SHIP ACTION

During the War of 1812 the Royal Navy lost three frigates, HMS *Macedonian*, HMS *Guerriere* and HMS *Java*, to the young United States Navy. This was a bitter blow to the pride of a nation with such a long and proud tradition. Captain Philip Broke knew that his ship HMS *Shannon* could not match the big American frigates in size and firepower, but gunnery *was* one thing he could do something about. During his seven years as captain of *Shannon* he worked his ship to a peak of fighting efficiency with an unrivalled regime of gun drill. Every day, with the exception of Sunday, his men were exercised at quarters and firing at a target.

In June 1813 *Shannon* engaged USS *Chesapeake* under Captain James Lawrence in an epic fight off Boston, the finest single-ship action in the age of sail.

After *Shannon* fired a devastating broadside into *Chesapeake* Lawrence fell wounded but continued to give orders to return fire. A vicious hand-to-hand fight ensued as Broke himself led a boarding party on to *Chesapeake*. Lawrence bravely urged his men: 'Don't give up the ship!' Three American sailors attacked Broke. He killed the first, but the second hit him with a musket and the third sliced open his skull before being overwhelmed.

The entire action lasted only 11 minutes, but its unequalled ferocity (a projectile hit *Shannon* every four seconds) left 148 American and 83 English sailors killed or wounded. Lawrence died of his wounds three days later. *Shannon*'s victory caused a sensation in America and England, and Broke returned to a hero's welcome. He eventually recovered from his wound but was unable to return to active service and was troubled with head pains for many years.

Broke's victory brought official recognition that in battle good gunnery is as important as bravery – and the subsequent establishment of the world's first school of naval gunnery in 1830 at HMS *Excellent,* moored off the northwest corner of Portsmouth dockyard. Her larboard broadside was positioned to face Fareham Creek so that the firing of guns would not trouble civilians ashore.

HMS Shannon *and USS* Chesapeake.

IN THE DOLDRUMS – in a state of depression.
DERIVATION: the Doldrums is a belt of winds between the trade winds of the northern and southern hemispheres. As ships passed through these latitudes there was often no breeze to fill the sails or cool the living spaces and they were becalmed in sweltering conditions, aimlessly drifting.

THE SEA LORD AND THE NOBLE SAVAGE

Omai was the first Tahitian to visit England, arriving on board HMS *Adventure* on 14 July 1774. In his early twenties, he was brought at his own request from the Society Islands by Captain Tobias Furneaux, listed on the ship's muster book as a supernumerary under the name Tetuby Homey. His family had once been wealthy landowners but had lost their property in tribal conflicts, and Omai, hoping the English might be able to help him seek revenge, had begged Furneaux to take him to 'Britannia'. In England Omai became an exemplar of the 'noble savage' propounded by philosophers such as Rousseau.

The eminent scientists Sir Joseph Banks and Dr Carl Solander, who were both familiar with the Tahitian language, took Omai under their wing and introduced him into society. He was personally welcomed by the First Lord of the Admiralty, the Earl of Sandwich. The sea lord entertained Omai at his country house, Hinchingbrooke, where guests experienced the novelty of feasting on meats cooked over hot stones Polynesian style. He took him on a tour of Chatham Dockyard and aboard HMS *Victory*, where Omai expressed great joy at seeing so large a ship. Omai was delighted with a suit of armour that his host had made for him by the artificers of the Tower of London.

The sea lord's protégé quickly became the toast of the town. He met George III twice and when first presented to the royal personage he declared, 'How do, King Tosh.' The monarch was so taken with the young man that he granted him a pension while he was in England. Omai dined with the great names of the day such as Samuel Johnson and Fanny Burney; he went to balls, the opera and attended the state opening of parliament. He loved indulging in various British pastimes such as shooting, skating and picnicking, was a frequent guest at Royal Society dinners and was painted by some of the great artists of the time, including Joshua Reynolds.

Omai returned to Polynesia in 1777, on the last of Captain Cook's voyages. He died there two years later, apparently of natural causes.

ACTUALLY . . .

Captain Digby in HMS *Africa*, along with another British ship, HMS *Conqueror,* took on the Spanish flagship *Santissima Trinidad* at the Battle of Trafalgar. With rigging and sails hanging over her sides and the firing ceased, it appeared that the Spanish vessel had struck her colours, the signal of surrender. Digby sent Lieutenant Smith with a party of seamen to take possession. In accordance with the code of honour observed in naval engagements of that time Smith was courteously received by the Spanish officers, who then coldly informed him that in fact they had not actually surrendered and had no intention of doing so. They went on to explain that they had merely paused in the fighting to supply more powder to the guns; Smith was escorted back to his ship's boat and allowed to return safely to *Africa,* which went on to seek other opponents. *Santissima Trinidad* eventually surrendered to another English warship, HMS *Neptune,* but sank in a storm the day after the battle.

> DON'T LIKE THE CUT OF HIS JIB – put off by a person's outward appearance. DERIVATION: for an experienced sailor the cut of a jib, a triangular sail on the foremast, was a characteristic indicator of the type of ship, and sometimes the nationality. French and Spanish ships often had their jibs cut very much higher than British ships.

WATCH THE WALL, MY DARLING, WHILE THE GENTLEMEN GO BY

In the days before income tax the government of England had to raise money however it could. In the eighteenth century there were over 2,000 items subject to customs duty. This was the heyday of the smuggler and large numbers of people were either directly or indirectly involved – to many it was a perfectly acceptable way of behaving. Some newspapers ran advertisements such as this one from a Sussex paper of 1785 offering: 'A very useful cart, fit for a maltster, ash-man, or a smuggler... and many articles that are very useful to a smuggler.' Not only did the authorities often turn a blind eye: some were happy to fill their own cellars with contraband goods.

Some smugglers have endeared themselves down the years. Harry Paulet was master of an English vessel trading in North America when he was taken prisoner by the French. He contrived a daring escape, carrying with him important official documents that he had stolen from his captors, and he handed these over to the captain of an English ship. The information they contained proved valuable to the navy, and with the reward money he was granted Paulet went back to England and promptly purchased a vessel that he used to run contraband across the Channel.

He was returning from France in 1759 when he spotted the French fleet leaving Brest, headed for England. Paulet threw over his helm and sailed to Admiral Hawke's squadron with the news. Upon hearing what he had to say the admiral told him that if he was right he would make his fortune, but if it was deceit he would hang at the yardarm. With Paulet on board the British set off and subsequently gained a decisive victory at the Battle of Quiberon Bay. Paulet's cash reward enabled him to retire in style, and for the rest of his life he took much pleasure in recounting these exploits at his local tavern.

Perhaps the most famous Cornish smuggler was John Carter, 'the king of Prussia', a nickname from a favourite boyhood game. He had his head-quarters in a remote inlet between Penzance and Helson, which became known as Prussia Cove. Carter was a devout Methodist who banned swearing on his smuggling vessels. He once suffered the indignity of having goods seized by the revenue men that he had promised to one of his regular customers. He broke into the customs house and reclaimed 'his' property but left everything else untouched. The matter was taken no further.

On the other hand, there were bands of smugglers who terrorised whole areas and were quite prepared to maim and murder to protect their inter-ests. The notorious Hawkhurst gang of Kent could raise 500 armed men in less than an hour to defend their goods, and the customs officers were unable to touch them.

Despite generous rewards offered, smugglers were rarely turned in to the authorities.

A SHIP HAS BEEN SIGHTED
in this quarter
ENGAGING IN THE UNLAWFUL ACT OF

SMUGGLING

whosoever can lay information
leading to the capture of this ship
or its crew
will receive a reward of

£200

From His Majesty's Government.
This 19th day of October 1782

'*I* HAVE NOT YET BEGUN TO FIGHT!'

John Paul Jones, one of the American navy's first heroes, was born in a humble gardener's cottage in Kirkbean, Scotland. He joined the merchant marine at 13 and sailed to the West Indies. In 1773 he was involved in an incident there in which a man was killed and John Paul, as he was then, fled to the United States, changing his name to John Paul Jones.

Commissioned into the Continental Navy, the new navy of the United States, he took part in several actions in the early stages of the Revolutionary War off the North American coast and also in raids on English shores. In 1776, on board *Alfred*, he hoisted by his own hand the first flag ever flown from a US warship, a yellow silk banner emblazoned with a rattlesnake. In his ship *Ranger* in 1777 he captured the British warship HMS *Drake*, the first man-of-war to surrender to a Continental Navy ship flying the Stars and Stripes. Jones became the toast of the French as well as the Americans for this action.

He then put to sea in *Bonhomme Richard* with a small squadron to harass British merchantmen. Jones encountered a Baltic convoy of 44 vessels, escorted by the frigate HMS *Serapis* under the command of Captain Pearson. After a furious four-hour battle, *Serapis* came alongside *Bonhomme Richard*, which had been badly damaged. Pearson hailed Jones and asked if he was surrendering, to be told: 'I have not yet begun to fight!' Then *Serapis* caught fire and Jones seized his chance and boarded her, taking the vessel. *Bonhomme Richard* sank shortly afterwards and Jones sailed in *Serapis* to the Texel, where he was welcomed as a hero.

Jones spent much of the rest of his life in France. In 1905, more than a century after his death in Paris, his remains were returned to the United States and entombed at the US Naval Academy in Annapolis, Maryland, where his shrine, permanently guarded by a duty midshipman, is open to the public.

John Paul Jones.

*N*OBLE FORBEARANCE

When the white ensign of HMS *Bellerophon* was shot away for the third time during the Battle of Trafalgar, Christopher Beaty, a yeoman of signals, refused to accept this affront to his ship. He hastily rummaged around for another one and then began to climb hand over hand up the mizzenmast with the flag wrapped around his shoulders. Almost instantly he was the target of enemy fire, but he pressed on doggedly. When he reached the top, he spread out the ensign and proceeded to attach the corners firmly to the shrouds so that it stood proud. At this point the French sharpshooters in the tops of *L'Aigle* suspended their fire in recognition of his courageous action and allowed Beaty to clamber back down unharmed.

> **COPPER BOTTOMED** – a pretty safe bet, often describing an investment. DERIVATION: in 1783 the Royal Navy started routinely sheathing the hulls of wooden warships with copper to prevent infestation from wood-destroying parasites such as the infamous gribble and teredo worms. This was seen to be very effective.

*S*EAMAN TO SAMURAI

In Japan William Adams became known as '*Miura Anjin*', the pilot of Miura, after the estate he was given in recognition of his services to his adopted country. An English navigator, Adams served under Francis Drake and was later recruited by the Dutch for their trading voyages to the East Indies.

In April 1600, after more than 19 gruelling months at sea, the merchantman *Liefde* anchored off Kyushu in Japan. Adams was among what remained of the crew, just 20 sick and dying men. Initially believed to be pirates, they were seized and incarcerated. Adams was nearly executed, but as the fittest of the prisoners he was brought to Osaka for questioning. A powerful feudal lord who would later become shogun took a liking to him, eventually making him a diplomatic and trade adviser and bestowing great privileges on him.

Adams supervised the building of several Western-style ships for the shogun, who conferred the rank and authority of a samurai on him. Although he had a wife and children in England, Adams married a Japanese woman and had another family with her, but he was forbidden to leave Japan.

In 1611 a letter from Adams was received at the London offices of the East India Company. As a result they began sending ships to the Far East to trade with Japan. Adams facilitated similar arrangements with the Netherlands and personally became involved in Japan's Red Seal trade, in which merchant sailing vessels conducted business with Southeast Asian ports under the authority of a red seal permit issued by the shogun.

One of the most influential foreigners during Japan's first period of opening to the West, William Adams died in Japan on 16 May 1620, aged 56. His life story inspired the character of John Blackthorne in James Clavell's *Shogun*.

Red Seal ship.

'*M*Y FIN'

Following his injury from a musket-ball at Tenerife in 1794, Nelson's right arm was amputated high up near the shoulder. The operation was performed without anaesthesia, and it is unlikely that he was given rum to dull the pain as alcohol was said to interfere with the clotting of the blood. Within a short time of the surgery he was issuing orders to his captains. The wound, however, took many months to heal as one of the ligatures used during the operation, which normally fell out after a few weeks, remained in the wound, causing continuing infection and intense pain.

The surgeons who performed the amputation and the doctors and apothecaries who cared for Nelson received special payment; he was reimbursed £135 1s. 0d. for his medical expenses.

Nelson sometimes experienced the sensation of a phantom arm. He nicknamed the stump his 'fin', and it was said that it twitched if he was agitated or angry. Officers would then warn: 'The admiral is working his fin, do not cross his hawse.'

Armless Jokes

Nelson sometimes joked about his affliction. On his arrival in Great Yarmouth in November 1800 the landlady of the Wrestlers Arms asked permission to rename her pub the 'Nelson Arms' in his honour. 'That would be absurd, seeing I have but one,' he replied. And when, at a levée at St James Palace, George III referred to his having lost his right arm, Nelson came back swiftly, 'But not my right hand,' and, turning to one of his companions, told the king, 'I have the honour of presenting Captain Berry.'

*S*OME PASSENGER . . .

Shortly after the Battle of Waterloo Napoleon Bonaparte surrendered – not to Wellington but to the captain of the ship that had dogged his steps for more than 20 years, HMS *Bellerophon* – 'Billy Ruffian'

to her crew. The ship sailed for England and dropped anchor at Torbay on 24 July 1815. Every effort was made to keep the famous man's presence a secret, and no one was allowed to come on board. However, a sailor dropped into the water a black glass bottle which was retrieved by some young boys in a small boat nearby. Inside the bottle was a rolled piece of paper with the electrifying message, 'We have Bonaparte on board!'

Once the word spread, the vessel was quickly surrounded by sightseers in anything that could float. Bonaparte even appeared on deck to greet the crowds. The British government was worried that the emperor might escape before they could work out what to do with him, so *Bellerophon* was hastily ordered to weigh anchor and sail to Plymouth, with its more secure harbour.

Needless to say people thronged there; at the height of the madness 10,000 people boarded 1,000 boats in an attempt to get a view of the most famous man in the world. Several even drowned in the frenzy.

The crew of *Bellerophon* hung notices over the ship's side as to their famous guest's movements: 'In cabin with Captain Maitland', 'Writing with his officers'...

Among the crowds were large numbers of pretty young women, naval officers, fashionably dressed ladies, red-coated army officers and smartly attired gentlemen. The men took off their hats respectfully when Napoleon showed himself, as he did every evening around 6 p.m. He commented on the beauty of the young ladies and appeared astonished by the size of the crowds.

On 7 August Napoleon was transferred to HMS *Northumberland* for exile in St Helena, where he died in 1821.

Bonaparte was proclaimed First Consul for Life in 1802. He crowned himself Emperor Napoleon I in 1804.

BONAPARTE,
Premier Consul.

SWINGING THE LEAD – skiving to avoid work.
DERIVATION: the depth of water under a vessel was measured by lowering a lead weight on the end of a rope over the side of a ship. It was necessary to twirl the line and shoot it ahead so that by the time the lead had sunk to the bottom the ship's headway would have brought the line perpendicular and the correct depth could be seen. Some seamen would make a great display of twirling the lead around their heads, pretending to be active rather than doing the job properly.

'BLACK DICK' TO THE RESCUE

Richard Howe was one of the larger-than-life figures in British maritime history. He spent 60 years as a professional sea officer, serving with great distinction in many of the famous fleet actions of the age. Howe was officially Lord Richard Howe of Langar Hall, but to the sailors of the fleet he was always just 'Black Dick'. There have been a number of explanations offered for this, his swarthy complexion being one. The fact that he was said never to smile unless a battle was about to begin may also have earned him his nickname!

On 16 April 1797, a mutiny began at Spithead, the chief naval anchorage near Portsmouth. Sixteen ships in the Channel Fleet raised the red flag of insurrection: their principal demands were for a rise in pay (which had not been changed for 150 years), a more equitable distribution of prize money and better victuals. The mutineers elected delegates from each ship to represent them.

When negotiations broke down between the two sides, George III personally requested Howe, who was held in very high regard by British seamen, to go down and talk to the mutineers. Although over 70 and suffering from gout and other ailments, he agreed. When First Lord Spencer asked the admiral who he wished to accompany him he replied simply, 'Lady Howe.'

They set out on 10 May on a wild and stormy night and arrived at Portsmouth the following morning. Howe left his wife at the governor's house and immediately set out by barge for Spithead. He came alongside HMS *Royal George,* the headquarters of the insurrection, and despite his infirmities he rejected all offers to help him come aboard and clambered up unaided. He called the ship's company to the quarterdeck and started to talk to them man to man, neither reproaching their conduct nor standing on his dignity. Several hours later he went to HMS *Queen Charlotte*. For three days he went from ship to ship – talking, listening, heaving his rheumaticky knees and gouty feet up and down ladders until he was so tired he had to be lifted in and out of his boat. But by the end he had achieved reconciliation on both sides, with a Royal pardon for all the mutineers, a reassignment of some of the most unpopular officers and a pay rise and better victualling for the seamen.

On 15 May there was a grand celebration in Portsmouth, and the mutineers' delegates marched in procession up to the governor's house accompanied by bands playing 'God Save the King' and 'Rule, Britannia'. The delegates were invited inside for refreshments, then appeared on the balcony with the Howes to huzzahs from the multitude, after which they set out together for the anchorage. On board *Royal George* Howe was given three cheers and the red flag of mutiny was pulled down; the other ships quickly followed. Later that day Lord and Lady Howe hosted a special meal for the delegates before they returned to their ships and reported for duty.

RICHARD FIRST EARL HOWE.

Nelson called Howe 'our great master in tactics and bravery'.

A WOMAN'S TEARS SAVED *VICTORY*

England's most iconic ship already had a long and proud history before her most famous role as Nelson's flagship at the Battle of Trafalgar in 1805. Although she was well over 40 years old, considerably past the normal life span of a ship of the line, she went on to further service in the Baltic and other areas. Her career as a fighting ship effectively ended in 1812. She was 47 years old, the same age Nelson had been when he died.

In 1831 she was listed for disposal, but when the First Sea Lord Thomas Hardy told his wife that he had just signed an order for this, Lady Hardy is said to have burst into tears and sent him straight back to the Admiralty to rescind the order. Curiously, the page of the duty log containing the orders for that day is missing.

Victory was permanently saved for posterity in the 1920s by a national appeal led by the Society of Nautical Research. To this day she is manned by officers and ratings of the Royal Navy and has now seen two and a half centuries of service, proudly fulfilling a dual role as flagship of the commander-in-chief naval home command and as a living museum of the Georgian navy.

HMS Victory.

OF UMBRELLAS AND URCHINS

 Jonas Hanway has two claims to fame – for introducing the umbrella to England and encouraging a life at sea for many thousands of men and boys.

Merchant, philanthropist and social reformer, Hanway travelled extensively. In Persia he was taken with a silk parasol and brought one back to England. It was light green outside, pink inside. Its carved handle had a joint in the middle so that it could fold and go into his coat pocket. Hanway was ridiculed for many years by hackney coachmen who thought it would cause them to lose income. Hanway stubbornly carried an umbrella through London for three decades and lived to see it become the standard accoutrement for a gentleman, even being called a 'Hanway'.

In 1756 Britain was facing a severe shortage of men in the navy as she found herself embarked on another war. Concerned about the manning crisis, Hanway called a meeting of London merchants and other interested parties at the 'King's Arms' on 25 June. He proposed that they set up an organisation that would provide practical encouragement to young men to volunteer for service at sea. He also saw this would be a way for the street urchins of London to escape their miserable conditions. Thus the world's first seafaring charity, the Marine Society, was born.

It offered sponsorship to 'all stout lads and boys, who incline to go on board his Majesty's ships, with a view to learn the duty of a seaman, and are, upon examination, approved by the Marine Society, [they] shall be handsomely clothed and provided with bedding, and... borne down to the ports... with all proper encouragement'.

By 1763 the Marine Society had recruited over 10,000 men and boys. In 1786 it commissioned the world's first pre-sea training ship, the sloop *Beatty*. Admiral Nelson became a trustee of the charity, and at the time of the Battle of Trafalgar 15 per cent of the navy was being supplied, trained and equipped by the Marine Society.

Today, a little over 250 years after Hanway's meeting in the 'King's Arms', the Marine Society, now merged with the Sea Cadets, continues to serve seafarers.

The Merchant Seamen's Office over the Royal Exchange, used as a Board Room by the Marine Society from July 15th 1756 to April 6th 1758.

Marine Society boardroom, 1756.

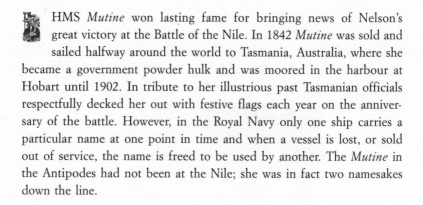

> BOW AND SCRAPE – being excessively servile.
> DERIVATION: an officer's cocked hat was known as a
> 'scraper' after its similarity to the wooden utensil of the same name
> used by the ship's cook. When greeting a superior officer it was
> customary for the junior officer to remove his headgear and bow.

Oops . . .

HMS *Mutine* won lasting fame for bringing news of Nelson's great victory at the Battle of the Nile. In 1842 *Mutine* was sold and sailed halfway around the world to Tasmania, Australia, where she became a government powder hulk and was moored in the harbour at Hobart until 1902. In tribute to her illustrious past Tasmanian officials respectfully decked her out with festive flags each year on the anniversary of the battle. However, in the Royal Navy only one ship carries a particular name at one point in time and when a vessel is lost, or sold out of service, the name is freed to be used by another. The *Mutine* in the Antipodes had not been at the Nile; she was in fact two namesakes down the line.

'The swedish knight'

Sir Sidney Smith was one of the most colourful characters of his time – vivacious, quick, daring and mercurial. He entered the Royal Navy in 1777 and soon distinguished himself in battle. He was made post captain at the age of 18. Between 1789 and 1791 he was an adviser to the king of Sweden in the maritime war with Russia. King Gustavus conferred an order of knighthood upon Smith, earning him the mocking nickname 'the Swedish knight' from his contemporaries, most of whom took against his flamboyance.

In 1799 Smith was given charge of the Turkish naval and military strength assembling to attack a French invasion force. He took command of two British warships at Alexandria, and when he heard that Bonaparte had stormed Jaffa on his way to Syria he quickly made his way to the walled city of Acre that stood athwart Napoleon's route for his advance into India.

There he put 800 seamen and marines ashore and mounted ships' guns on the ramparts. Over the next six weeks his courage and determination inspired the Turkish defenders against overwhelming odds. Napoleon gave up his ambitions and the siege was raised on 20 May.

A grateful Britain gave Smith a pension of £1,000 a year, along with the thanks of both houses of parliament. The sultan of Turkey presented him with the *chelengk*, the plume of triumph, which he delighted in wearing. The magnitude of the defeat for the French was such that years later in lonely exile Napoleon said of Smith: 'That man made me miss my destiny.'

After Acre, however, Smith never achieved such accolades again. Although highly intelligent, his career was constrained by a reputation for impulsiveness and unconventionality. One admiral found him 'as gay and thoughtless as ever', and Wellington called him 'a mere vaporiser'.

Finally, in December 1815, Smith was awarded a British knighthood – he was no longer just 'the Swedish knight'. He attained the rank of admiral in 1821 and in his later years campaigned vigorously for the release of Christian slaves from captivity in North Africa.

Sir William Sidney Smith depicted at the Battle of Acre, his greatest triumph. The painting is by John Eckstein, who also recorded the Royal Navy's incredible achievement in fortifying Diamond Rock in 1804.

MAINSTAY – someone of great support and help.

DERIVATION: in a sailing ship a stay is part of the standing rigging that supports a mast. Stays take their name from the mast they support; a mainstay is thus a crucial component on any vessel.

CHALK AND CHEESE

 Louis Infernet and Jean Lucas were arguably the two most courageous French captains at the Battle of Trafalgar, but they could not have been more different in appearance.

Infernet stood 1.8 m tall and was built like a prize fighter. He spoke in a rough Provençal dialect; one of his colleagues said of him, '*Infernet parle mal, mais il se bat très bien*' – Infernet speaks badly, but he fights damn well. Commanding *Intrépide*, he fought one of the most gallant actions of the battle, at one point under fire from four or five British warships simultaneously.

Lucas, on the other hand, slightly built and standing under 1.5 m tall, was the smallest officer in the French fleet. His ship *Redoutable* became sandwiched between HMS *Victory* and HMS *Temeraire* and endured a relentless pounding from their broadsides. Lucas and his crew fought heroically as decks were torn open, guns shattered. When he eventually surrendered just one mast remained upright. Their butcher's bill was horrendous – 88 per cent of her crew were either killed or injured.

SEA-GOING SYMBOL OF PRIDE

 Bluenose was a deep-sea fishing schooner that won a special place in the hearts of all Canadians during the depths of the Great Depression, an admiration that continues to this day. As one newspaper observed: 'Her name is a household word. She has knit Canada together.'

It all began with a small item in the sports page of a New York paper in 1919 announcing that the America's Cup race had been postponed because of a blow that would barely tickle the sails of a saltbank schooner. The men of the fishing fleets of Gloucester in Massachusetts and Lunenburg in Nova Scotia were outspoken in their scorn.

Competition between the two communities had always been fierce and here was the perfect excuse to have a race between real working schooners. In 1920 the International Fishermen's Race was organised, and that year the schooner *Esperanto* out of Gloucester defeated the *Delewana* of Lunenburg and took the trophy to New England. The cousins in the north were not going to take this sitting down, however, and in the following spring a challenger bearing the name *Bluenose* was launched, a 'Bluenose' being a resident of Nova Scotia.

She was constructed by traditional methods using local timbers, and had, of course, the sturdy build of a working schooner. Her lines were sweet, however, and she was fast, achieving her best speed under a strong blow beating to windward. In 1921 she raced twice against *Elsie* in the waters off Halifax. *Bluenose* took both races with a good margin and even reduced sail to match the American vessel during one race when her opponent temporarily got into difficulty. *Bluenose* was a 'witch on the wind' and nothing could catch her.

Undefeated in all the International Fishermen's trophy series held between 1921 and 1938, she became an enduring symbol of Canada's maritime spirit. In 1929 the Canadian Postal Service issued a distinctive blue stamp to honour the vessel's racing record, and in 1937 she appeared in full sail on the Canadian dime.

Bluenose's fame was not confined to North America and Canada. She officially represented her country at the World's Fair in 1933 and the Silver Jubilee of King George in 1935.

Sadly, she met her demise in 1946 when she foundered near Haiti, some say as the result of a voodoo curse. But her name lives on. The reverse side of the Canadian dime still proudly bears an image of the schooner. Meanwhile *Bluenose II,* a daughter ship launched from the same shipyard and built by many of the same men who worked on the original *Bluenose,* carries on the tradition of sailing ambassador for Canada.

The Bluenose, Canada's favourite stamp. In 2001 a Bluenose first day cover sold for nearly C$4000.

NOT A MAN LOST

 William Bligh has not had a good press, and is thought of as one of the most tyrannical and cruel captains ever to command a ship.

This largely false accusation has overshadowed his achievement of one of the most remarkable feats of seamanship and survival of all time, his near 6,400-km open-boat voyage across the vast and empty western Pacific with scant provisions and only very basic navigation equipment.

On 28 April 1789 there was a mutiny aboard Bligh's ship HMS *Bounty*. Fletcher Christian and the master-at-arms burst into Bligh's cabin. They had come to the end of their tether after his continuing vicious insults and vowed to cast him and his supporters adrift, thereby condemning them to a lingering death.

Along with 18 men who remained loyal to him Bligh was forced into the ship's launch, an open boat 7 m long and 2 m wide. They were allowed some basic navigation equipment (but no charts), a mast, several sails, some food and water and a few empty barricoes or small casks.

Initially they headed to the nearby island of Tofoa for more food and water, but there one man was killed by natives and they were forced to flee. Some of their provisions were lost in the rush to escape.

Bligh decided to make for the Dutch trading settlement on Timor, 6,400 km away. From the start he established strong discipline. He divided the men into watches and had them fashion a log line so they could estimate speed. Stormy weather forced them to throw overboard anything that could be spared so that the overcrowded launch did not ride so dangerously low in the waves.

Food and water was strictly rationed. Using coconut shells Bligh fashioned a pair of scales and used a pistol ball to weigh each man's meagre rations of one twenty-fifth of a pound of ship's biscuit, three times a day. This was supplemented on occasion with half an ounce of pork in the evening, and a few spoonfuls of rum or wine. As the voyage progressed the rations were shortened to an issue twice a day. Occasionally they caught a booby, a small sea bird, and divided it between them, giving the blood to the weakest.

Not one man was lost on the voyage after leaving Tofoa. On 14 June they reached Timor and their epic journey of 47 days was over.

The National Maritime Museum at Greenwich acquired three relics from this heroic boat voyage – the bullet Bligh used to measure the rations, a horn beaker for drinking water and the coconut shell from which he ate his rations and on which Bligh had carved his name and the following words: 'The cup I eat my miserable allowance out.'

 UNDER THE WEATHER – being indisposed.
DERIVATION: one of the most uncomfortable lookout positions in a sailing ship was at the bow on the windward or weather side. When the elements got rough the poor unfortunate stationed there was continuously soaked with cold, biting sea spray, and when he finally came off watch he looked a sorry sight.

$\mathcal{P}$ATENT BRIDGE FOR BOARDING FIRST-RATES

During the Battle of St Vincent in 1797 Horatio Nelson captured two enemy ships in a manner that was unique in the history of the Royal Navy.

Although his ship HMS *Captain* was badly damaged, Nelson was determined to fight to the end. Two Spanish ships *San Nicolas* and *San Josef* lay off afoul of each other nearby. Nelson initially ordered *Captain* put alongside *San Nicolas* and prepared to lead the boarding party himself. It was extremely unusual for a flag-officer to take such an action, but Nelson was no ordinary commander.

Captain's cathead became entangled with the stern gallery of *San Nicolas*, in effect making a bridge to the ship. Nelson led his men out along the cathead and into the Spanish captain's cabin. Under fire from the Spanish officers the boarders stormed on to the quarterdeck. There, Nelson received the swords of the Spanish officers in surrender.

After securing his rear, he then led his boarding party in another furious assault into the main chains and up the sides of *San Josef*. Leaping over the bulwark and down to the quarterdeck he rapidly took possession of the second ship.

Then, in a scene immortalised by painters, the Spanish officers came forward in strict order of seniority to hand their swords to Nelson. As he accepted them he passed them to seaman William Fearney, who, Nelson later recorded, 'put them with the greatest sang-froid under his arm'.

THE EXECUTION OF AN ADMIRAL

In April 1756 Admiral John Byng sailed from England with ten ships of the line tasked with assisting in the defence of Fort St Philip in Minorca against the French. After fighting an indecisive four-day action Byng decided that his force was insufficient either to renew the attack or to relieve the fort and he sailed to Gibraltar, in effect leaving Minorca to the enemy. This aroused a storm of protest.

On his return to England Byng was confined in Greenwich while the government considered its options. An angry populace wanted answers and there were burnings of Byng effigies. For six months a debate raged, and finally a court martial was convened. Under the Articles of War he could face the death penalty.

The court martial was held in Portsmouth on 28 December 1756 and Byng was charged with failing to do his utmost to save Minorca. On 27 January he was found guilty and, despite the fact that two vice-admirals refused to sign the warrant, he was condemned to death. Clemency lay in the hands of the king, but George II considered Byng a coward, as did popular opinion.

At noon on 14 March 1757 a great crowd gathered on the ramparts of the town and along the shore. Byng spent the morning calmly surveying the onlookers through a telescope from his flagship *Monarch*. 'I fear many of them will be disappointed,' he said; 'they may hear where they are, but they cannot all see.' Dressed in light clothes he walked firmly to the quarterdeck, where a cushion rested on a pile of sawdust. Kneeling there, and refusing a friend's offer to tie a bandage over his eyes he said, 'I am obliged to you, sir; I thank God I can do it myself.' In an act of cold-blooded courage, he dropped a handkerchief himself as a signal to the party of marines to fire.

Incentive Scheme

Byng was the only British admiral ever to suffer this fate. The French writer Voltaire took delight in including it in his satirical tale *Candide*, published in 1759. The hero, visiting Portsmouth, sees a man being executed on board a ship and, on asking why, is told that in England it is thought a good idea to execute an admiral from time to time – '*pour encourager les autres*'.

The epitaph on Byng's tombstone read: 'To the perpetual disgrace of public Justice... The Honourable John Byng, Admiral of the Blue, fell a martyr to political persecution... at a time when courage and loyalty were insufficient guarantees of the honour and lives of naval officers.'

PICKLE'S POSTMAN NEARLY PIPPED AT THE POST

 It took over two weeks for the Admiralty to receive the news of Britain's great victory at the Battle of Trafalgar – and the tragic death of Horatio Nelson on board HMS *Victory*.

Admiral Collingwood, who took over as commander-in-chief, wrote his dispatches on the morning of the day after the battle, but owing to a storm and the immediate needs of the fleet it was four days before he was able to send them.

On 26 October 1805 Collingwood summoned Lieutenant John Lapenotiere, in command of the schooner *Pickle,* the fastest vessel then at his disposal, and ordered him to sail to Plymouth with the dispatches and with all haste proceed to the Admiralty. If there were difficulties he was to make the first port he could and then go on to London.

Being the bearer of official news of victory was a much-coveted role, as there would inevitably be promotion and financial reward. But in carrying out his duties, Lapenotiere was nearly frustrated by the actions of another naval officer.

En route back to England HM sloop *Nautilus* was sighted and Lapenotiere told her commander John Sykes the momentous news. Sykes immediately sailed for Lisbon to inform the British consul, then unknown to Lapenotiere he headed directly for London. An unofficial race for glory had begun!

On 4 November Lapenotiere was forced by weather conditions to land at the Cornish port of Falmouth. He hired a chaise for the first stage of his overland dash, improvising a broomstick for a flagpole on which he flew a Union Jack above a tattered *tricolore*. Not long after, Sykes landed at Plymouth, further along the coast, and he too hired a carriage.

Lapenotiere's journey of 425 km took 21 changes of horses and carriages and his expenses amounted to £46 19s. 1d. – nearly half of his annual salary.

Finally the coach clattered into the Admiralty courtyard at 1 a.m. in the morning of 6 November, 36 hours after Lapenotiere had left Falmouth. It was a neck and neck 'race' to the very end as Lapenotiere entered the vestibule of the Admiralty less than one hour before Sykes. Most of the officials had long since retired for the night but William Marsden, secretary to the Navy Board, was on his way to his private apartments having just finished work in the board room. Lapenotiere handed over the dispatches with the simple words, 'Sir, we have gained a great victory. But we have lost Lord Nelson.'

Lapenotiere was later presented to King George, who bade him accept a token and presented him with the closest thing to hand, a silver cruet.

Pickle's captain became inextricably linked with the death of Nelson for ever, while Sykes is now nothing more than a historical footnote.

George III.

SLUSH FUND – in the political sphere, a special account for fighting elections circumventing the usual process of auditing. DERIVATION: one of the perks of being a sea cook in the Royal Navy was the slush, the fat skimmed off the cooking liquor as salted meat was boiled in vast copper vats. This murky fluid was solidified and then sold to be used for lubricating rigging aloft.

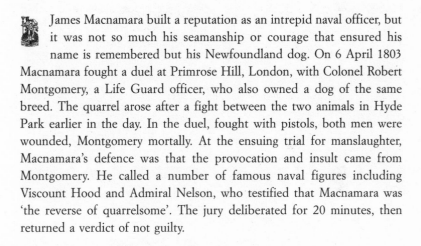

DUEL OVER A DOG

James Macnamara built a reputation as an intrepid naval officer, but it was not so much his seamanship or courage that ensured his name is remembered but his Newfoundland dog. On 6 April 1803 Macnamara fought a duel at Primrose Hill, London, with Colonel Robert Montgomery, a Life Guard officer, who also owned a dog of the same breed. The quarrel arose after a fight between the two animals in Hyde Park earlier in the day. In the duel, fought with pistols, both men were wounded, Montgomery mortally. At the ensuing trial for manslaughter, Macnamara's defence was that the provocation and insult came from Montgomery. He called a number of famous naval figures including Viscount Hood and Admiral Nelson, who testified that Macnamara was 'the reverse of quarrelsome'. The jury deliberated for 20 minutes, then returned a verdict of not guilty.

'IF I WERE NOT THE RUSSIAN TSAR . . .'

Peter the Great was the founder of the Russian navy and the first tsar ever to venture outside his country's borders. From a very young age he was keen on ships and sailing, and he developed an abiding and very much hands-on interest in shipbuilding.

In 1697 the young tsar began his 'Grand Embassy', a fact-finding mission to look into ways of modernising his country. After studying shipbuilding in Holland Peter made it known to King William III that he now wished to see something of England's maritime capability. When Tsar Peter arrived in England in 1698, the king provided a number of attendants to accompany him and arranged for him to have every assistance, as well as excellent accommodation.

Peter was given the use of Sayes Court, a fine house adjacent to Deptford royal shipyard; conveniently its back gate led directly into the yard. The tsar loved to watch the craftsmen at their operations and would pick up tools and work alongside them himself. Often he wore the dress of a common shipwright as he roamed about the shipyard, although with his height of just over 2 m he was hardly inconspicuous.

Peter not Great as a Tenant

The owner of Sayes Court, the diarist John Evelyn, was initially delighted to have such a famous tenant, but was later incensed at the damage Peter and his companions caused to his property. Furnishings were ruined and many of the fine paintings had been used as shooting targets. What particularly appalled Evelyn, a keen gardener, was the harm done to his fine holly hedges by a riotous game in which Peter and his friends were raced around the grounds in wheelbarrows. Eventually the King's Surveyor recommended that Evelyn be paid £350 in compensation.

When Peter visited the dockyard at Portsmouth the king arranged for the fleet to put to sea and staged the first-ever mock battle in the Channel in his honour. Peter was so delighted that he said: 'If I were not the Russian tsar I would have wished to be an English admiral.'

While in Portsmouth he asked to see the arrangements used for hanging sailors who had been given a death sentence. There was nobody scheduled for execution at the time, so Peter offered one of his own men for a demonstration. The offer was politely declined.

When the time came for Peter to return to Russia the king presented him with *Royal Transport*, a lavishly furnished yacht armed with 24 guns. The tsar set off with a number of English naval craftsmen whom he had engaged to help him build up his own navy.

Peter's deep connection with shipbuilding and the sea continued throughout his life. He became a competent marine architect and shipwright; some said he was the best in Russia. One of the first major projects in his new imperial capital at St Petersburg was the construction of an Admiralty building, where he would spend at least one or two hours every day.

Tsar Peter had courage to match his physical stature. In November 1724, aged 52, he leapt into freezing water and worked tirelessly through the night to rescue 20 sailors from a ship that had been grounded. Shortly afterwards he contracted a fever and died.

*T*HAT WAS THE YEAR THAT WAS!

> Come, cheer up, my lads! 'Tis to glory we steer
> To add something more to this wonderful year...
> Heart of oak are our ships
> Jolly tars are our men...
> We'll fight and we'll conquer again and again

Annus mirabilis, 1759, during the Seven Years' War, was possibly the most significant year in British history since 1066. It was immortalised by the playwright David Garrick in 'Heart of Oak'.

In August Admiral Boscawen engaged the French fleet at Lagos, off the southern coast of Portugal. After his flagship was disabled he shifted his command to another ship. When the boat taking him there was hit by a round shot and a strake was stove in, Boscawen calmly plugged the hole with his wig. He continued the chase all night and captured three French ships and destroyed two, returning to Spithead with his prizes and 2,000 prisoners. The victory prevented France from sending an invasion force from Brest.

On the other side of the globe, Quebec, the key to the conquest of upper Canada, was captured by Wolfe and Admiral Saunders in the autumn. The superb charts of the area produced by James Cook enabled the fleet to bring formidably sized ships up the St Lawrence River. Seamen landed guns ashore and hauled them up to an area overlooking the city. While Wolfe took Quebec, the fleet lay off the city, denying supplies and reinforcements to the defenders.

In November Admiral Edward Hawke caught up with Admiral Conflan's fleet at Quiberon Bay, where they planned to embark an army of 20,000 men and invade England. Hawke hoisted the signal for 'general chase'. His ships crowded on sail to pursue the enemy into the bay as darkness was falling, using the French ships as markers to try to keep clear of the treacherous rocks in the shallow waters of the bay. Hawke's master urgently warned him of the peril ahead, to which Hawke replied, 'You have done your duty in pointing out to me the danger. Now lay me alongside the enemy flagship.'

The French did not believe the British would follow them on to a lee shore, but they did. In a fierce action, the French lost seven ships of the line with 2,500 men dead. Two British ships ran aground and were wrecked, but it was a decisive strategic victory which once again averted the threat of invasion.

This glorious year, which became known as 'the year of victories', also saw a keel laid in Chatham Dockyard for a new warship called *Victory* – and the first birthday of the man who would lead her at Trafalgar.

In May 1759 James Cook surveyed the approaches to Quebec. The work, done within range of the French guns, often had to be carried out at night.

BETWEEN THE DEVIL AND THE DEEP BLUE SEA
– having two equally undesirable alternatives.

DERIVATION: part of maintenance of a wooden ship was the application of hot pitch to the devil, a seam between the waterways, the timber fashioning which ran along the side of the ship from the bow to the stern. The task involved being swung out precariously in a bosun's chair over the rolling sea.

$\mathcal{A}$ BRAVE MAN'S SWORD

 Admiral Adam Duncan and Admiral Jan de Winter were both over 1.9 m tall and proportionately well built – and their physical size matched their prowess as sea warriors.

The two Goliaths faced each other at the Battle of Camperdown in 1797. A furious engagement, echoing the fights of the seventeenth-century Dutch wars, was maintained by both sides until De Winter's flagship was overwhelmed. Admiral Duncan refused to accept his sword in surrender saying, 'I would much rather take a brave man's hand than his sword.'

De Winter was conveyed to England and treated with great courtesy by his captors. When Duncan heard that De Winter's wife had suffered a stroke he quickly arranged for his repatriation. In accordance with the ancient customs of parole and exchange De Winter gave his word never to fight the English again and left the sea for diplomacy. However, after the Peace of Amiens Napoleon abolished this gentlemanly code of behaviour and De Winter returned to the sea.

Admiral Jan de Winter. He died in 1812 and was buried in the Panthéon, Paris.

THE *L'ORIENT* COFFIN

One of the most unusual battle trophies of all time must be the coffin made from the wreckage of the French flagship *L'Orient* that blew up at the Battle of the Nile in 1798. It was presented to Nelson by Captain Hallowell of HMS *Swiftsure* on 23 May 1799. Hallowell had retrieved a large section of her mainmast and instructed his carpenter to fashion it into the macabre gift. Nothing was used in its construction that had not come from *L'Orient* and an accompanying note certified to this fact. It is not clear why Hallowell had this coffin made in the first place, nor why he waited ten months before he sent it to Nelson. The two were friends who had seen service together, and perhaps Hallowell feared the effect of all the praise showered on Nelson after his celebrated victory at the Nile.

A covering letter sent with the coffin stated: 'My Lord, herewith I send you a coffin made of part of the *L'Orient*'s mainmast that when you are tired of this life you may be buried in one of your own trophies – may that period be far distant is the sincere wish of your obedient servant.'

While his officers were appalled, Nelson was amused and for some time he had the coffin standing upright against the bulkhead of his cabin, behind the chair he sat on for dinner. Subsequently it accompanied him as part of his luggage during his long overland journey home to England with Emma and William Hamilton in 1800. In London it was stored with Nelson's agents, Messrs Marsh, Page and Creed. During a brief period of leave in the autumn of 1805, just before the Battle of Trafalgar, Nelson visited them and instructed that the certificate of authenticity be engraved on the lid, adding, 'I think it is highly probable that I may want it on my return.' Was this cryptic comment a presentiment of his early death?

'OLD JARVIE'

John Jervis, who was to become Admiral of the Fleet and Earl St Vincent during the Napoleonic Wars, joined the navy at 13 with no money apart from his pay. His father would not honour a draft of £20 he had drawn on him, but Jervis paid back the debt, shilling by shilling over three years. This left him so poor that he could not afford to pay his mess expenses, so he did not eat with other midshipmen or associate with them in any way, except for official duties. Instead, he made friends with the lower ranks and developed a deep knowledge of their ways.

Throughout his 73 years in the navy 'Old Jarvie' was much loved by common seamen. His nickname reflected his aggressive, rather bull-like appearance; a 'jarvie' was a hackney driver inured to plying his trade in all weathers.

The sailors appreciated his taut but fair discipline; almost alone of all the captains he never exceeded the maximum sentence allowed of one dozen lashes. His concern for the health of his crews was legendary, he instigated well-equipped sick bays, and a special hospital ship kept company with the fleet to care for the severely sick and wounded.

On occasion individual kindnesses further endeared him to the sailors. In one famous incident Petty Officer Roger Odell playfully jumped off the foreyard fully clothed to go swimming – forgetting he had his entire life savings of £70 in his pocket. Back aboard Odell broke into tears on finding his pounds reduced to pulp. Jervis admonished the man for crying, but said he was a fine seaman and replaced the money from his own pocket.

Jervis loathed waste and inefficiency. It was said he knew the exact quantity of stores on each ship down to the last box of nails and ball of twine and would audit a ship's stores without notice. He did much to reduce the corruption within the navy. Jervis was also fanatic about sail drill and gunnery practice in all weather.

'Old Jarvie' was not always popular with the officers or their wives. When he was appointed to the command of the Channel Fleet he put a stop to the easy-going regimen whereby captains could spend a good deal of their time ashore at social functions. The story is told of one lady at a dinner party giving as a toast, 'May his next glass of wine choke the wretch!'

His devotion to the navy and belief in its supremacy was summed up by his statement in the House of Lords when the threat of invasion from France was at its height: 'I do not say, my Lords, that the French will not come. I say only they will not come by sea.'

Earl St Vincent, naval hero of rigorous self-sufficiency and professionalism.

> KNOW THE ROPES – have skill and experience.
> DERIVATION: it took years to understand the function of,
> and be able to locate and control, the multitude of ropes (or lines,
> as most of them were known to mariners) in a man-of-war. This
> ability was considered so important that a skilled seaman's
> discharge papers were marked 'knows the ropes'.

ALL DOWN TO BISCUITS AND A BOULDER

HMS *Pique,* a frigate designed by the famed naval architect Sir William Symonds, left Quebec in September 1835. As she sailed out of the mouth of the St Lawrence River a thick fog descended. The ship hit a reef and was battered relentlessly against the rocks all night. In the morning her captain Henry Rous finally freed her by jettisoning 20 cannon and a large quantity of water to lighten the ship.

As soon as she got into deep sea a gale blew up and she began to take in water badly. To add to her troubles *Pique*'s rudder was carried away and the only way she could be steered was by trimming sails and trailing hawsers. A temporary rudder was eventually fitted, but this too was soon swept off. Unable to go about on the right tack for England she eventually managed to signal a passing French brig who obliged by heaving her bodily around.

Pique was now taking in 1 m of water an hour and the pumps were manned day and night. Deep below in the bowels of the ship the carpenter worked tirelessly to plug what leaks he could.

The gale continued throughout the whole voyage, and when *Pique* finally limped into Portsmouth a dockyard inspector said he had 'never seen any ship enter port in such a state'. She was found to have virtually no keel left, and in some places the torn floor timbers were wafer thin. A large hole was discovered to have been plugged by a sack of ship's biscuits swollen with the sea water, and a huge rock 4 m in circumference was snapped off in the hull, stopping up a monstrous cavity midships.

Rous later told Symonds, 'Your beautiful ship has had the hardest thumping that ever was stood by wood and iron.'

The very rock that was embedded in *Pique* may be seen today in the grounds of the Portsmouth Historic Dockyard.

Promoted to admiral in 1852, Henry Rous was a lover of horse racing from boyhood. He did much to bring fairness to the sport by devising a weight-for-age scale.

'WHERE SHALL I FIND A MATCH FOR THIS?'

Irishman Jack Spratt was a good-looking, high-spirited master's mate aboard HMS *Defiance* at the Battle of Trafalgar. During the action Captain Durham ordered him to lead a boarding party to take *L'Aigle*, but the ship's boats were found to be shot through. Undeterred, Spratt called the boarders to follow him, snatched a cutlass and leapt overboard to swim to *L'Aigle,* where he soon found himself in fierce hand-to-hand fighting. He was attacked by several soldiers, and having just fought them off and deflected a bayonet thrust at him by another he was severely injured in the leg with a musket ball.

Meanwhile *Defiance* had managed to come alongside and the boarding party leapt to the deck. Through the smoke one of the first people Captain Durham spotted on *Aigle* was Spratt, his bloody leg dangling over the rail. 'Captain, poor old Jack Spratt is done up at last,' he called out, and he was hauled back aboard *Defiance.*

Spratt was taken to the surgeon, who wanted to amputate the leg, but he refused. The surgeon appealed to Durham to intervene and order the operation. The captain tried to reason with Spratt, but he merely held up his good leg and said, 'Never! If I lose my leg, where shall I find a match for this?'

Spratt was landed at Gibraltar, where he was hospitalised for four months. He kept his leg but was lame for the rest of his life. He achieved the rank of commander and retired to Devon, where he was often seen riding on a small Dartmoor pony. Despite his incapacity Spratt retained his swimming skills and when he was nearly 60 years old he swam a 23-km race for a wager and won.

H.M. Sloop INVESTIGATOR. 1802.

No 3/50   Sea Power   Geoffry C. Ingleton

Chapter 2.

Sea Explorers,

DISCOVERERS &
INVENTORS

Sea Explorers, DISCOVERERS & INVENTORS

Introduction

The first European sea voyages that impelled the West into an unparalleled age of world discovery and trade were launched by Portugal's Prince Henry the Navigator in the early fifteenth century. Before that voyages had been coastal, keeping always within sight of land. Other nations quickly followed the Portuguese, notably the Spanish, the Dutch and the English. For the often illiterate sailors crewing the ships, these voyages were frightening journeys into the unknown. Many had fears that they would perish horribly in the infamous Green Sea of Darkness, a terrifying place of lurking monsters and boiling seas.

But more than a century before Christopher Columbus set sail, China mounted seven great exploration voyages under Zheng He, the Admiral of the Western Seas. He sailed to western Asia, Africa and Arabia, visiting some 40 countries. Zheng He's voyages heralded a momentous period of exploration and trade for China.

In the Golden Age of Sail inventive minds were tackling every kind of problem, from how to plot your position to ship-to-shore rescue. One of the most poignant of their achievements was Henry Winstanley's lighthouse on the Eddystone reef, the first to be built in the open sea. It was a true feat of human invention and withstood a fiercely unforgiving environment for five years. During the titanic storm of 1703 Winstanley was on it with his men. When the tempest abated he and his lighthouse had completely vanished.

Engraved world map, from a book printed in 1628 compiled by Francis Drake's nephew.

ADMIRAL OF THE WESTERN SEAS

Zheng He was a Muslim born in China's mountainous province of Yunnan in 1372. The Ming Dynasty had been established in 1368, bringing to an end Mongol rule. At the age of 11, Zheng He was captured and castrated when Ming forces were sent to Yunnan to destroy the last stronghold of the old regime. His reputation for bravery had been noted, however, and he was assigned to a royal household where over time he became very powerful. As an adult he was described as brave and quick-witted, a tall, heavy man with clear-cut features, long earlobes and a stride like a tiger.

When his master seized the Peacock Throne and became Emperor Yong Le, he made Zheng He 'Admiral of the Western Seas'. Over the next three years an incredible flotilla of sailing ships was built under his direction, ushering in a golden period of exploration and trade for China, and making her the most advanced seafaring nation in the world.

Seven great exploration fleets commanded by Zheng He set sail between

1405 and 1433; they were the mightiest the world had ever seen. The first carried 28,000 people in around 300 vessels, including the treasure ships which were of extraordinary size. Nine-masted, 120 m long and 49 m wide, each ship could carry more than 1,000 passengers. *Nina, Pinta* and *Santa Maria,* the three ships of Columbus built more than a century later, would all fit easily inside a *single* Chinese treasure ship.

In addition to sailors and soldiers there were merchants, astrologers, craftsmen and priests on board. Zheng He's fleet had a number of technological innovations, including magnetic compasses and watertight compartments, which would not be seen in European vessels for hundreds of years. There were even on-board vegetable patches.

Zheng He sailed to western Asia, Africa and Arabia, visiting 40 countries. Some speculate that he reached America and even circumnavigated the world. Others believe he touched on the shores of Australia. Of all the wonders he brought back, the most exciting to his countrymen was a giraffe from Somalia.

The Admiral of the Western Seas died in 1433 on the return voyage of the seventh expedition. Thereafter there were no more heroic voyages: a new Chinese ruler ushered in 500 years of isolation; the logs of the seven remarkable voyages were destroyed, and the giant treasure ships abandoned and left to decay.

The Chinese artist Shen Du, a favourite of Emperor Yong Le painted the giraffe Zheng He brought back from the east coast of Africa.

THE BEACON OF LIGHT

Until the end of the seventeenth century one of the great threats facing shipping heading to Plymouth on the southern coast of England was the isolated and treacherous Eddystone reef, 23 km directly offshore. Much of the hazard is underwater, creating complex currents, and extraordinarily high seas are often kicked up when conditions are very windy. In 1620 Captain Christopher Jones, master of *Mayflower* described the reef: 'Twenty-three rust red... ragged stones around which the sea constantly eddies, a great danger... for if any vessel makes too far to the south... she will be swept to her doom on these evil rocks.'

As trade with America increased during the 1600s a growing number of ships approaching the English Channel from the west were wrecked on the Eddystone reef.

King William III and Queen Mary were petitioned that something be done about marking the infamous hazard. Plans to erect a warning light by funding the project with a penny a ton charge on all vessels passing initially foundered. Then an enterprising character called Henry Winstanley stepped forward and took on the most adventurous marine construction job the world had ever seen.

Work commenced on the mainly wooden structure in July 1696. England was again at war, and such was the importance of the project that the Admiralty provided a man-of-war for protection. On one day, however, HMS *Terrible* did not arrive and a passing French privateer seized Winstanley and carried him off to France. When Louis XIV heard of the incident he ordered his release. 'France is at war with England, not humanity,' said the king.

Winstanley's was the first lighthouse to be built in the open sea. It was a true feat of human endeavour. Work could only be undertaken in summer and for the first two years nothing could be left on the rock or it would be swept away. There was some assistance from *Terrible* in transporting the building materials, but much had to be rowed out in an open four-oared boat in a journey that could take nine hours each way.

Winstanley's lighthouse was swept away after less than five years, during the great storm of 1703. Winstanley was on it at the time supervising some repairs – he had said that he wished to be there during 'the greatest storm that ever was'.

The next lighthouse was built by John Rudyerd and lit in 1709. Also made largely of timber and with granite ballast, it gave good service for nearly half a century until destroyed by fire in 1755. During the blaze the lead cupola began to melt, and as the duty keeper, 94-year-old Henry Hall, was throwing water upwards from a bucket he accidentally swallowed 200 g of the molten metal. No one believed his incredible tale, but when he died 12 days later doctors found a lump of lead in his stomach.

John Smeaton, Britain's first great civil engineer, was the next to rise to the challenge of Eddystone. He took the English oak as his design inspiration – a broad base narrowing in a gentle curve. The 22-m high lighthouse was built using solid discs of stone dovetailed together. Work began in 1756, and from start to finish the work took three years, nine weeks and three days. Small boats transported nearly 1,000 tons of granite and Portland stone along with all the equipment and men.

The Smeaton lighthouse stood for over 100 years. In the end it was not the lighthouse that failed; rather that the sea was found to have eaten away the rock beneath the structure. In 1882 it was dismantled and brought back to Plymouth, where it was re-erected stone by stone on the Hoe as a memorial, and where it still stands. It had already been replaced by a new lighthouse, twice as tall and four and a half times as large, designed by James Douglas, which now gives mariners a beacon of light visible for 22 nautical miles.

Rudyerd's Eddystone Lighthouse.

> THE COAST IS CLEAR – activity can proceed
> unhindered. DERIVATION: in the heyday of smuggling a boy
> led a white horse along a cliff as a signal, visible at night, that there
> were no Revenue men about and it was thus safe for smugglers to
> land contraband cargo brought over from France by sea.

A VOYAGE THAT CHANGED HISTORY

In the early sixteenth century the Portuguese had a virtual monopoly on the only known sailing route to the Moluccas (part of modern-day Indonesia), eastwards around Africa. But if another way could be found to these fabled islands of spices, there would be great riches to be had.

On 10 August 1519 after nearly a year of preparation the Armada of Molucca, five small ships under the command of Ferdinand Magellan, left Spain on a daring quest to find a different route to the Spice Islands by going in the opposite direction, around South America. This would be through waters completely unknown to civilisation.

Almost three years to the day after they had departed, the armada returned with proof positive that the world could be circumnavigated by sea. But it was not Magellan who had achieved this incredible feat – he had not even contemplated it; his plan was to return from the Moluccas the same way he had come.

When the expedition stopped in the Philippines for food and water en route to the Spice Islands, Magellan became embroiled in a dispute with local tribes and met his death there at the hands of a local chieftain, Lapu Lapu. With the loss of Magellan there was in-fighting between the ships and a succession of commanders vied to take up the mantle. From the outset the expedition had been dogged by misfortune and in the end only one ship, *Victoria*, made it back to Spain. Out of the original 265 men who had set out in 1519 just 18 survived, half-dead from starvation and disease.

Although Magellan's achievements are enormous – he crossed a fearfully unknown ocean, one far vaster than Columbus had sailed, and opened the way for future exploration of what in effect was half the planet – it was a man now almost forgotten by history, Juan Sebastian Elcano, who had brought *Victoria* safely back to Spain sailing westwards from the Moluccas, thereby becoming the first man to sail around the world.

Charles I of Spain feted Elcano and presented him with a pension and coat of arms with the inscription *'Primus Circumdedisti Me'* – you were the first to encircle me.

Detail from a map by
Flemish cartographer
Abraham Ortelius –
Magellan's ship Victoria.

NOT JUST A WORD-GRINDER

He has been called the father of modern nautical fiction, but Frederick Marryat had a number of strings to his bow including an adventurous career around the world as a naval officer, serving in the Mediterranean, the West Indies, the East Indies and North America.

In an age when swimming was not a widespread skill he saved the lives of more than a dozen sailors by diving into the sea to rescue them and was awarded a gold medal from the Royal Humane Society.

In 1817 Marryat published his *Code of Signals for the Merchant Service*, an adaptation of Sir Home Popham's navy signalling system of 1803. Unlike the Popham system, which needed several numeral flags per hoist to denote a word, the Marryat system simplified things with alphabetical flags, thereby using three times fewer. As well as being adopted by the merchant marine it was used by many others, and served as the basis for the *Universal Yacht Signals* code published by the Royal Yacht Squadron in 1847.

While still at sea Marryat wrote and had published a three-volume novel, *The Naval Officer, or Scenes and Adventures in the Life of Frank Mildmay*. He left the navy in 1830 to concentrate on his literary career and went on to write over ten more books, including a number of children's titles.

His code of signals for the merchant navy was so popular that it was in use unchanged until 1879, even though it had been officially replaced by the *International Code of Signals* in 1857, which was largely based on Marryat's original conception.

The Language of Flags

 Flags were an important means of communication between ships. However, it wasn't until towards the end of the nineteenth century that the International Code of Signals was widely adopted, enabling ships of all nations to signal each other and be understood. This code was even designed so that the flags could be read by the colour-blind.

Previous systems were individual to a particular fleet or squadron, and users required a unique codebook in which to look up the meaning. These were weighted with lead so they could be thrown overboard in case of capture.

Nelson's famous signal at the Battle of Trafalgar, 'England expects that every man will do his duty', required 13 separate flag hoists, 32 flags in total. The admiral initially wanted to use the word 'confides', but agreed to change it to 'expects' in order to use fewer flags.

Colours, the national ensign flown at the masthead at sea, had special significance. It was acceptable to fly false colours, i.e. those of some other country, but not to fire on another ship without first hoisting one's true colours. If a ship's colours were flown upside down, it was the signal for distress. When a vessel was captured, the colours of the victor were hoisted above those of the prize.

In large sea battles, frigates were stationed to one side out of the gun-smoke to act as 'repeaters', passing on signals from the commander-in-chief. Both sides agreed not to fire on these frigates.

Flags, however, did have drawbacks. If the wind blew them end-on they could not be read; battle-haze often hid them; they were not visible at night; and only a limited number of flags can be flown at one time, so complex signals were impossible.

Captains were often thus forced to fall back on the tactic of 'speak the ship' – foam up alongside and bellow at each other with a speaking trumpet.

A SQUARE MEAL – substantial repast. DERIVATION: sailors ate their food off square wooden plates with a raised edge called a fiddle. This design was to stop food falling off the plate and to set a limit on the amount of food taken. If a seaman overfilled the plate he was said to be 'on the fiddle' and could be punished.

FLOWERS FROM THE 'END OF THE WORLD'

Henry the Navigator was the man chiefly responsible for Portugal's heroic age of exploration between the 1430s and the 1550s, but he never actually set sail on any of these great voyages of discovery. Born in 1394 he was the third child of King John I of Portugal. Contemporary records describe him as a person who did not indulge in luxuries, was softly spoken and never allowed a poor person to leave his presence empty-handed.

Henry established a maritime think-tank and gathered the great minds of the day around him. Under his patronage a number of expeditions sailed south to extend the boundaries of the known world. But in the fifteenth century the red sandstone cliffs of Cape Bojador off the west coast of Africa was seen as the point beyond which there was no return. There the seas crashed into the cliffs in constant fury, fearsome waterspouts erupted and dust storms howled off the cliff tops.

According to popular belief, past the cape lay the end of the world, the Green Sea of Darkness, an area where the sun was so close to the Earth that a person's skin would turn black, the sea boiled, ships caught fire and monsters lurked waiting to smash the ships and eat the sailors. Henry did not believe any such nonsense, but up until 1433 he could entice no seaman to pass Cape Bojador.

Henry's persistence did finally pay off. He persuaded Gil Eannes, who had turned back after starting a previous voyage, to make a second attempt. This time Eannes reached the cape, skirted around its deadly hazards and then worked his way inshore until he reached the coast, where he landed and picked flowers. When he returned he announced that beyond Cape Bojador there was in fact no Green Sea of Darkness.

Prince Henry died in 1460, having transformed European expansion and trade from the old land routes to new sea routes in the Southern Ocean. By the end of the sixteenth century Lisbon was the European hub of commerce with the Far East.

Henry the Navigator.

$\mathcal{M}$ERCATOR, MAPS AND MARS

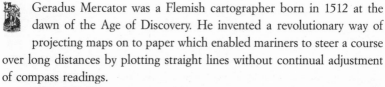

Geradus Mercator was a Flemish cartographer born in 1512 at the dawn of the Age of Discovery. He invented a revolutionary way of projecting maps on to paper which enabled mariners to steer a course over long distances by plotting straight lines without continual adjustment of compass readings.

In 1544 Mercator was put in jail for seven months on trumped-up charges of heresy, probably because the Dutch had ambitions to be a world sea power and were anxious to prevent such maps getting into the hands of others.

Mercator later moved to the German Duchy of Cleves, and in 1569 he used his radical projection plan to construct a map of the world. Although his map was to change the future of cartography and navigation profoundly, initially it received scant attention. However, this was the age of Queen Elizabeth, and rival nations were groping for the navigational key to an ocean empire. Seers like John Dee were sent over to bring back such secrets and they duly returned with instruments and the new charts.

At the time these were too advanced for the ordinary mariner, and it was not until some years after Mercator's death in 1594 that his projection was accepted for navigational use at sea on any significant scale. By about 1640 it was widespread and this continues to be the case on today's navigation charts. And in the twenty-first century it is Mercator projections that NASA are using to map Mars!

Mercator's legacy did not stop there. He was one of the first mapmakers to cut up maps and bind them inside boards, later coining the term 'atlas' to refer to such collections.

Geradus Mercator.

*I*CY GRAIL

The search for the Northwest Passage, a shorter shipping route from Europe to the wealth of the Orient via the ice-bound waters of the Arctic, began in the late fifteenth century with the voyages of the father and son explorers, John and Sebastian Cabot.

Finding this fabled passage preoccupied the Elizabethan imagination. Among the heroic maritime explorers of the age who sought to connect the Atlantic and Pacific Oceans were Martin Frobisher, Humphrey Gilbert and John Davis.

Gilbert, who wrote a treatise on the Northwest Passage in 1566 that inspired many later explorers, disappeared off the coast of Labrador on 9 September 1583. From the deck of *Squirrel* he hailed another expedition ship, *Golden Hinde*, calling across to them in encouragement, 'We are as near to heaven by sea as by land.' Later that evening somewhere in the darkness his ship was swallowed up by the sea, with the loss of all souls.

Henry Hudson made four momentous voyages in search of the Northwest Passage. On 22 June 1611, during his last voyage, he suffered a mutiny aboard. He and seven of his crew, plus his young son, were set adrift in a small boat and died in the Arctic bay to which his name has been given.

Interest then waned for many years. In 1744 the British government offered a prize of £20,000 (over £3 million today) to the first person to discover the Northwest Passage. The search was on again in earnest and a series of naval expeditions, including James Cook's third great voyage of exploration, were mounted. Much of the Arctic area was charted but the Northwest Passage remained elusive. The last official naval expedition was the famous voyage of Sir John Franklin, who sailed into Lancaster Sound in 1845 in HMS *Erebus* and HMS *Terror* and was never seen again.

Over the course of the next decade over 30 search parties were sent out to solve the mystery of Franklin's disappearance. This was largely due to the persistence of his wife Jane, who herself sponsored four expeditions, including the final one in 1857 led by Captain Leopold McClintock. One of the searchers in the McClintock expedition, Robert McClure, found sad relics of Franklin's expedition. He also gained official recognition for the proof of the reality of the Northwest Passage.

The truth of the Franklin tragedy has now emerged. During the winter of 1846–7 Franklin's two ships became trapped in thick ice. Franklin died in June 1847 and by April of the next year 21 more had perished in the bitter conditions from a combination of starvation, scurvy and lead poisoning (from their canned food). They probably resorted to cannibalism as their situation became ever more desperate.

Ironically, more people died looking for Franklin than perished on his final voyage.

The fabled passage was not successfully navigated until the twentieth century, when Roald Amundsen completed a full transit by sea in his tiny vessel *Gjoa* in 1906.

As the Arctic ice melts with global warming the Northwest Passage may yet turn out to be the great trade route connecting two oceans that maritime explorers sought for four centuries.

John Franklin.

PRESS ON – push ahead with all speed, regardless of comfort. DERIVATION: at sea a captain would often crowd on as much canvas as conditions allowed in order to complete a voyage in the shortest possible time. Thus rigged, a ship would be said to be 'under a press of sail', her bow pushed into the waves, resulting in a wet trip.

THE MAN WHO PUT AUSTRALIA ON THE MAP

If you look at a map of Australia you are looking at the memorial of the great navigator and cartographer Matthew Flinders. In the course of his work he survived shipwreck and disaster and was imprisoned for many years as a spy. Although his life was short, his achievements made him one of the most important naval explorers of his time.

Flinders circumnavigated the lonely continent in 1801–03. He had previously charted Tasmania with George Bass in 1798–9, demonstrating it was an island separated from the mainland by a strait of water. Flinders proved that the east coast, charted by James Cook in 1770, was part of the same land mass as the west, which had been surveyed by the Dutch navigators during the seventeenth century.

As he was returning to England in 1803, not knowing that England was at war with France again, he put into Mauritius for repairs to his ship *Cumberland*. The French governor believed he was a British spy and he was incarcerated there for over six years. In 1804, detained under close confinement, he drew the first map of Australia. Towards the end of his time in Mauritius he wrote *A Biographical Tribute to the Memory of Trim*, the charming story of the seafaring cat who accompanied him during his circumnavigation of Australia.

During his voyage around the great continent Flinders had noted abnormal behaviour of the compass needle, and to correct for this he proposed that a length of iron bar be let into the deck, with its upper end level with the compass card in the binnacle. Although such compensating devices were not used until the second half of the nineteenth century they are called Flinders bars in his honour and are an integral part of ships' compasses even today.

When Flinders returned to England he had not seen his wife Anne for nine years and was in poor health as the result of his imprisonment.

However, he immediately began work on *A Voyage to Terra Australis*, which became widely read and gave the name Australia, which Flinders favoured, general currency. The governor of New South Wales used it in his dispatches to England and recommended to the Colonial Office that it be officially adopted. In 1824 the Admiralty decreed that the continent should officially be thus known, but Flinders did not live to see this as he died, just 40 years old, the day after his seminal work was published in 1814.

HM *sloop* Investigator, *in which Flinders circumnavigated Australia.*

'*H*E VANISHED TRACKLESS INTO THE BLUE IMMENSITY'

In 1785 Louis XVI of France commissioned a great voyage of exploration, a four-year expedition across the Atlantic Ocean and into the Great South Sea, as the Pacific Ocean was then known, before returning to France. It was to be led by Jean-François de Galaup, Comte de La Perouse, one of the country's most eminent naval officers. The project was heralded as France's most ambitious maritime endeavour; during its circumnavigation every field of science was to be studied. Louis wanted to secure a rank for France alongside Britain, then the world's leading seafaring nation, and personally gave instructions, specifying the itinerary and objectives.

No efforts were spared in provisioning the expedition's two frigates *La Boussole* and *L'Astrolabe*. As well as charts and navigation instruments they took a portable observatory and gifts for natives including 570 kg of glass beads and 50,000 sewing needles. Competition was keen for the 400 berths. Among the applicants was a 16-year-old second lieutenant from the military academy at Paris, a Corsican named Napoleone di Buonaparte; he was not selected.

Although most of La Perouse's naval career had been spent fighting the British, as an explorer he received their support and cooperation thanks to an act of humanity during the American War of Independence. La Perouse had destroyed the British forts in Hudson Bay but spared the lodgings of the British fur traders, leaving them food to survive the harsh winter. His actions were not forgotten, and when he was about to launch his expedition the British agreed to cooperate in his scientific quest. A French go-between was given access to James Cook's charts and surveys. When La Perouse left France he carried with him two compasses that had gone around the world with Cook, a gift of the Royal Society. He treated them with great veneration as he was a huge admirer of Cook.

La Perouse set sail for South America in August 1785 and entered the Pacific in early 1786. In September 1787 he stopped to take on water at Samoa, where natives killed 12 of his men including the captain of *L'Astrolabe*.

The two frigates sailed into Botany Bay at the end of January 1788 where La Perouse was surprised to find a British squadron – they had just founded Australia's first colony. La Perouse took the opportunity to send reports and letters home with some of the departing English ships.

On 10 March *La Boussole* and *L'Astrolabe* left Australia heading northeasterly. They were never seen again. The Scottish essayist Thomas Carlyle later wrote of La Perouse: 'He has vanished trackless into the blue immensity.'

In September 1791, six years after La Perouse had left, Rear Admiral d'Entrecasteaux came looking for him with two ships. They combed the Pacific and in May 1793 spotted smoke rising from the interior of an island to the northeast of Australia. D'Entrecasteaux was convinced he had found survivors of the expedition, but treacherous reefs forced him to leave without sending a search party ashore. D'Entrecasteaux died shortly after, and revolutionary France had other concerns: she was locked in war with much of Europe. No further rescue expedition was sent by the French. Louis XVI while being led to the guillotine is said to have asked whether there was any news of La Perouse.

It was not until 1826 that Peter Dillon, an Irish captain, found enough evidence to piece together the events of the tragedy, which was confirmed by the later investigation of the underwater remains of *La Boussole*. Both ships had been wrecked on the reefs off the island of Vanikoro, southeast of New Guinea, *La Boussole* first. *L'Astrolabe* had been unloaded and taken apart. One group of men, probably from *La Boussole*, were massacred by the local inhabitants. Some of the surviving sailors built a two-masted craft from the wreckage of *L'Astrolabe* and left westward about nine months later, but what happened to them is unknown. Two men, one a 'chief' and the other his servant, had remained behind, but their fate was never established.

> LOSE YOUR BEARINGS – not know where you are.
> DERIVATION: before modern navigation aids arrived, a ship's position when in sight of land was determined by the intersection of the compass bearings of two objects ashore. If one of these points of reference was obscured, the position of the ship would be unknown.

$\mathcal{H}$OW FAST ARE WE GOING?

During the great voyages of discovery by Columbus and others, sailors would arrive at a measure of their speed by dropping a chip of wood or some other material into the water and counting in seconds how long it took the ship to pass by it and then looking up special conversion tables. This method was still used on some Dutch ships at the end of the eighteenth century.

A more precise method came with the invention of the common log in the 1570s. This was a triangular piece of wood called the log-ship attached to a long line, knotted at regular intervals, which a sailor threw overboard, counting the number of knots that ran out within 30 seconds. This provided a record of the ship's speed in 'knots', a measure used to this day. A knot is 1.852 km per hour.

Various other improvements were tried, but it was not until 1802 that the first successful self-recording log was patented by Edward Massey, a clock and watchmaker in Newcastle. Massey's log recorded the distance travelled on a series of dials which could be read when the log and its line were retrieved from the sea. It proved very accurate and was used extensively at sea for much of the nineteenth century.

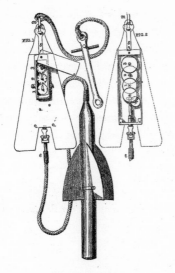

The instrument was based on a small rotator dragged in the water; motion was transmitted to a recording mechanism on the ship's rail.

Massey's log

TWO STORMS, TWO MEN

The inhabitants of coastal communities commonly witnessed the fury of the sea when sailing ships snapped their anchor cables in gales and broke up, their doomed passengers often tantalisingly close to the safety of the shore.

Two storms in 1807 were the catalysts to the work of the pioneers of ship-to-shore rescue, Englishmen George Manby and Henry Trengrouse. They lived at opposite ends of the country – Trengrouse in Cornwall and Manby in Norfolk.

On 18 February the gun-brig *Snipe* foundered off Great Yarmouth. The ship was carrying French prisoners and women and children. George Manby was among the helpless onlookers trying to shut out the screams of the drowning as the waves crashed over the ship. Sixty-seven perished within 55 m of the shore and more bodies were picked up along the coast. In the same year, on 29 December, Henry Trengrouse witnessed the fate of the doomed HMS *Anson* in Mount's Bay, Cornwall. She had been sailing to France to join a blockade of the French fleet when she ran aground in a storm only 90 m from shore. People along the shore watched as some 270 sailors made it to safety using the ship's masts as bridges to the beach, but to the horror of the onlookers more than 60 of the crew, including her captain, drowned.

Appalled at the loss of life so close to shore, both men came up with proposals for rescue apparatus; the ideas were similar but used very different methods to propel a line from shore to ship. Manby used a mortar to fire a lead ball with a line attached which would enable a rescue boat to be hauled between ship and shore. He subsequently replaced the recovery boat with a canvas cot and then developed a lightweight mortar which enabled apparatus to be carried on horseback. Trengrouse used a rocket rather than a mortar.

The first recorded rescue using the Manby contraption took place on 18 February 1808, when a party commanded by Manby himself saved the crew of the brig *Elizabeth* 140 m off Great Yarmouth. The Navy Board began to supply it to various stations around the coast, and 239 lives were recorded to have been saved with the device.

In 1818 Trengrouse demonstrated his apparatus to the Admiralty, who found his model superior to Manby's for ship-to-shore rescue work. They suggested that a specimen apparatus be placed in every dockyard, so that naval officers might become familiar with it. In the same year Trinity House recommended that it be carried on all its vessels. The government ordered 20 sets but then decided to have the Ordnance Board manufacture them. Trengrouse was paid £50 compensation and received a personal letter from Alexander I of Russia in recognition of the usefulness of his apparatus. He was awarded several medals and received 30 guineas from the Society of Arts, but apart from that no financial reward for his invention.

Improved rockets were later invented by John Dennett and Colonel Boxer, and the rocket completely superseded the mortar. To this day it still plays a role in ship-to-shore rescue.

Engraving depicting a stranded Indiaman, along with different rescue techniques of the nineteenth century.

TAKEN ABACK – jolted by unpleasant news, at a momentary loss. DERIVATION: a very real danger for a sailing ship was a sudden shift in the wind or an unexpected squall striking the ship from a different direction. The sails could be blown back against the masts, resulting in serious damage, possibly even leaving the ship helpless.

$\mathcal{S}$AVED FROM THE NOOSE BY HIS OWN HAND

The Matthew Walker, the first knot to bear a man's name, is used to keep the end of a rope from fraying. It is tied by unravelling the strands of a piece of rope, knotting the strands together, then laying up the strands together again. It may also be used for tying several separate cords, in order to keep them together in a bundle.

We may never know who Matthew Walker was but the story goes that he was a boatswain in the Royal Navy who found himself sentenced to death by a judge who had once been a sailor himself. For some reason the judge offered Walker a full pardon if he could show him a knot that he could neither tie nor untie. Walker called for 10 fathoms of line and retired to his cell, unlaid the rope halfway, put in a special knot and then laid up the rope again to the end. The judge was unable to undo the rope and Matthew Walker happily secured his freedom.

Matthew Walker knot.

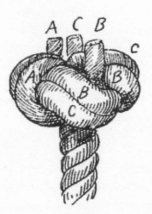

'OLD PURCHASE'

John Schank was a British sailor who was very skilled at mechanical design and constructed a cot fitted with pulleys that allowed it to be adjusted by the person lying in it. This won him the nickname 'Old Purchase', from the navy term for using a block and tackle to gain mechanical advantage.

Schank was one of the tiny handful of sailors who made the transition from the lower deck to flag rank. He joined the Royal Navy at an early age as an able seaman and ended his career as an admiral. As a young lieutenant during the American War of Independence he was placed in charge of local building of ships to battle the revolutionaries on the Great Lakes.

He was the first person in the western world to advocate the use of a keel that would slide through the centre of the boat and could be raised when not in use. On his return to England, Schank convinced the navy of the value of adjustable keels, and a number of vessels incorporating this feature, most notably *Lady Nelson*, were built. She was sent on a two-year expedition to chart the southeast coast of Australia, and was involved in the founding of a number of settlements there, including Melbourne and Hobart.

However, the sliding keels did have some problems with leakage and jamming, and for a time they went out of favour. Captain Molyneaux Shuldham came up with some modifications in 1809. He was a prisoner of war held by the French in Verdun, but he smuggled out a model of what he called his 'revolving keel'. It was exhibited at the Adelaide Gallery in London, where it came to the notice of three brothers from New Jersey, who in 1811 patented it in the US as the 'centre-board'.

This was quickly taken up and became a standard feature on 80 per cent of America's enormous coastal fleet. In due course American yachts-men saw its advantages, but few British racers took it on. An accident in 1876 was a tragic setback, however. *Mohawk*, a 43-m schooner, had her precarious 1.8-m draught made safe by a gigantic 9.5-m centre-board. Anchored off Staten Island during the preliminaries of the America's Cup, she was just setting sail for a leisure cruise when she was hit by a squall. Her centre-board had not been lowered and she capsized and sank; the vice commodore of the New York Yacht Club and all his guests died.

More improvements came over the years, and now the centre-board, based on Schank's pioneering idea of a sliding keel, is standard fitting on yachting craft.

Schank died on 6 February 1823, Fellow of the Royal Society and Admiral of the Blue. Mount Schank and Cape Schank, Australia, were named in his honour in 1800 by Lieutenant James Grant during his exploratory voyage while commanding *Lady Nelson*.

Woodcut of Lady Nelson.

WINDFALL – an unexpected stroke of good fortune.
DERIVATION: a sailing ship close in to land could sometimes encounter a strong gust of wind blowing down and away from high land. Canny captains would try to take advantage of this to maximise their speed.

*B*USHNELL'S *TURTLE*

The first submarine attack in the world occurred in 1776, against HMS *Eagle*, Lord Howe's flagship, while it was anchored in New York harbour. It was carried out by a one-man submarine called *Turtle*.

The submersible craft was the invention of American patriot David Bushnell and was an egg-shaped barrel built of oak reinforced with iron bands and fitted with an observation dome. The craft's dimensions were 2.3 m by 1.8 m. Once in the water the turtle floated just below the surface with its small conning tower exposed. It was propelled manually, the operator steering with his right hand while with his left he turned a crank connected to the propeller. The turtle had an oversized wood screw sticking up from the top with its handle inside the vessel's chamber. Attached to this screw was a waterproof fuse leading to a mine fastened to the outer hull.

On 7 September 1776 Sergeant Ezra Lee boarded *Turtle*. The plan was that he would manoeuvre the submarine under the warship and then manually drill the screw deep enough into the keel of the enemy ship to anchor it, detach both the screw and the mine, set the fuse burning and move away as quickly as possible.

But the mission was not successful; Lee was unable to penetrate the copper-plated hull of the ship.

Bushnell abandoned *Turtle* and concentrated on other inventions. In 1787 he mysteriously disappeared from his home. It was not until nearly ten years later that he was discovered to have moved to Georgia and become a professor, using the name David Bush.

A replica of *Turtle* was made for the 1976 US Bicentennial.

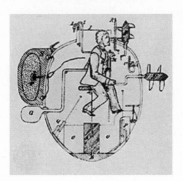

Drawing of a cutaway view of Bushnell's Turtle made by Lt Cdr F. M. Barber in 1885 from a description left by Bushnell.

SIMPLY THE BEST

There have been many outstanding maritime explorers – Columbus had great practical skill, Magellan pushed the bounds of discovery to unknown lands, Dampier was a keen observer of natural history and native peoples of the regions he visited. But in Captain James Cook these skills were united to a degree unmatched by any other in history.

Cook was born in very humble circumstances in 1728; his father was an agricultural day labourer. Cook had the good fortune of having a benefactor in Thomas Skottowe, the local lord of the manor. He helped with his education and later with an introduction to the Admiralty. Cook initially went to sea in the merchant navy and then joined the Royal Navy, where he worked his way up to the position of master in 1757.

Cook's brilliant work in charting the entrance to the St Lawrence River was crucial in the success of the British assault on Quebec. It allowed General Wolfe to make his famous stealth attack on the Plains of Abraham and helped bring Cook to the attention of the Admiralty. This led to his commission in 1766 as commander of HM Bark *Endeavour* for the first of his famous voyages.

The three voyages of discovery that he made between 1768 and his death in 1779 set new standards in navigation and surveying. He dispelled the myth of a Great Southern Continent, established that New Zealand was two islands and discovered and charted the eastern coast of Australia to a high degree of accuracy. The many scientists and artists who accompanied Cook collected invaluable data for numerous branches of study.

'Common Friend to Mankind'

Cook was a wise and respected captain and his contributions were widely recognised during his lifetime. In 1779, when the American colonies were at war with Britain, Benjamin Franklin wrote to captains of American warships at sea recommending that if they came into contact with Cook's vessel to:

'not consider her an enemy, nor suffer any plunder to be made of the effects contained in her, not obstruct her immediate return to England by detaining her or sending her into any other part of Europe or to America; but that you treat the said Captain Cook and his people with all civility and kindness... as common friends to mankind.'

Cook was killed ashore in Kealakekua Bay, Hawaii, in a fight with the natives. His body was burnt and the flesh stripped from the bone, following local funerary rites for a tribal elder. His skull and some arm and leg bones were later buried at sea, but many smaller bones were taken as prized artefacts. In 1824 King Kamehameha II repatriated Cook's remains to Britain, together with an arrow allegedly carved from one of Cook's leg bones. However, DNA tests have proved that the arrow is of animal, not human origin.

The legacy of Captain Cook lives on in his charts, which were adopted in their entirety by the Admiralty Hydrographic Department and have only ever been refined since then.

'*T*HE GENTLEMEN MUST HAUL AND DRAW WITH THE MARINERS'

 Francis Drake was born on a small farm in Devon in about 1540. He became one of the great Elizabethan sea explorers and adopted as his motto '*Sic Parvis Magna*' – great achievements from small beginnings.

In person he was stocky, with red hair and beard, and the ability to talk straight to anybody. Some called him an arrogant upstart but he was immensely courageous and energetic, and an inspiring leader of men. At one point he famously proclaimed to his crew: 'I must have the gentlemen to haul and draw with the mariners, and the mariners with the gentlemen.' This established professionalism at the core of the Royal Navy.

In 1580 Drake became the first English sea captain to circumnavigate the globe. By the time he returned to Plymouth in September of that year he had rounded Cape Horn through the strait named after him, sailed up the coast of Peru, ballasted his ship with Spanish gold and silver, landed on the shore of California, crossed the Pacific, reached the East Indies and the Spice Islands and sailed back via the Cape of Good Hope.

So vast was the treasure that he brought back with him that it was reckoned to meet the cost of an entire year's government. It was destined for the royal coffers, but Queen Elizabeth privately told Drake to take £10,000 for himself and the same for his crew.

Drake devoted much time to civic affairs and politics, but whenever he could he returned to sea. He boasted of 'singeing the King of Spain's beard' after an audacious raid on Cadiz in 1587 and a year later played his part in the defeat of the Spanish Armada, after coolly completing a game of bowls on Plymouth Hoe.

Buccaneer at the Bar

When in London Drake was sometimes a visitor to the Honourable Society of the Middle Temple, one of the inns of court. The high table in the hall consists of three 8.8-m planks of a single oak, reputedly a gift from Elizabeth I, cut down in Windsor Forest and floated down the Thames. The members of the inn still dine there as they did one evening in August 1586 when Drake, just back from a successful expedition against the Spaniards, was rapturously congratulated by all around the table. The hatch cover of his galleon *Golden Hinde* was later used to make the present 'cupboard', the table on which new barristers sign the roll book after being called to the Bar.

Drake captures a Spanish treasure-ship.

DELIVER A BROADSIDE – give a forceful rebuke that ends all further discussion. DERIVATION: a broadside was the simultaneous firing from one side of the ship of every cannon that could be brought to bear on the enemy. In a three-deck ship of the line with 50 guns or more this meant a considerable weight of ironmongery!

*F*ATHER OF METEOROLOGY

Robert Fitzroy captained the famous second survey voyage of HMS *Beagle* in which Charles Darwin developed his revolutionary theory. This association with one of the world's most influential men has somewhat overshadowed the contributions Fitzroy made to weather science.

During the first voyage Captain Pringle Stokes committed suicide at sea and Lieutenant Robert Fitzroy was appointed as *Beagle*'s captain. In February 1829, the new commanding officer found his ship blown on her beam-ends by a sudden violent squall. Only great skill in seamanship saved the day, but two crewmen had been swept from the rigging and drowned.

There had been a sharp drop in barometric pressure just before the squall, and Fitzroy's traumatic experience prompted him to wonder if a more systematic means could be devised to forecast bad weather. In 1843 he suggested that barometers be distributed along the coast of Britain to provide early warning of storms, but nothing came of this.

In 1854 the Board of Trade created a Meteorological Department and Fitzroy was made its superintendent. In 1857, by now an admiral, Fitzroy designed a simple robust 'Fishery Barometer' (which soon became known as the Fitzroy barometer) on which were inscribed weather lore rhymes such as 'When rise begins after low, squalls expect and clear blow'. With the financial assistance of a number of philanthropists he distributed 100 of the barometers to various seafaring centres and lifeboat stations.

Despite his efforts, in 1859 a well-found ship, the iron-clad steam clipper *Royal Charter*, sank in a storm off the Welsh coast resulting in nearly 400 deaths. The tragedy led to calls for the Meteorological Department to extend its activities by not only collecting weather statistics but also using the new telegraph network to send storm warnings to coastal centres, albeit the storms were probably already in progress. Fitzroy went further and developed his department into a unit for producing 'weather forecasts', a term he had coined in 1855.

By 1861 Fitzroy had in place a comprehensive system for getting out weather information and storm warnings which he coordinated from his London office. He then went on to produce a daily weather forecast, something no one had ever seriously attempted to do, which was published in *The Times*. However, the forecasts inevitably attracted attention when they were wrong and Fitzroy was subjected to public ridicule and condemnation in the House of Commons.

Fitzroy worked himself into the ground in his efforts to improve the quality of his forecasts. Going deaf and suffering from exhaustion and depression, on 30 April 1865 Admiral Fitzroy committed suicide at his Surrey home. It was a tragic echo of the fate of the captain of HMS *Beagle* from whom he took over.

In 2002, when the shipping forecast sea area 'Finisterre' was renamed to avoid confusion with the Spanish sea area of the same name, the new name chosen by the Meteorological Office was 'Fitzroy' in honour of their founder.

HMS Beagle *in the Straits of Magellan.*

Where are we?

Since the early days of sail mariners had been able to calculate latitude (their north–south position) by measuring with instruments the angular height of a star or the sun above the horizon. But a reliable way of calculating longitude (their east–west position) remained elusive until the late eighteenth century. As vessels undertook longer voyages this became an increasing problem. The loss of some 2,000 seamen in October 1707 when Sir Cloudesley Shovell's fleet sailed to disaster on the Scilly Isles brought clamours for a solution.

In 1714 the government of Great Britain offered a prize of £20,000 to anyone who could provide a solution to the problem of how to calculate longitude at sea. To administer and judge it a Board of Longitude was set up. The task was to invent a means of finding longitude to an accuracy of 30 nautical miles after a six-week voyage to the West Indies.

John Harrison was a Yorkshire carpenter by trade. He had only a limited education but developed a keen interest in machinery. Legend has it that at the age of six he was confined to bed with smallpox and was given a watch to amuse himself. He spent hours listening to it and carefully studying its moving parts. Harrison set out to tackle the problem of longitude in the most direct way – by attempting to produce a reliable clock that would not be affected by temperature, humidity and the rigours of being at sea. The idea was to be able to compare local time to that of Greenwich time, to which the chronometer would be set, and thus find the ship's longitudinal position. It would take him 30 years of development and experimentation.

In 1735 Harrison completed the first of his timepieces, T1. It was heavy and cumbersome, but he continued his work, encouraged by an award of £500 from the Board, and fired by the gritty determination of a Yorkshireman. After two more versions, T2 and T3, Harrison completed his fourth timepiece in 1759, and with T4 he hoped to claim the prize. This was demonstrated to fall well within the accuracy range specified by the contest. However, there was disagreement within the Board and delays for further testing.

Harrison began work on T5, which he sent to George III to test, whose interest in science was well known. The king was pleased with its accuracy and appealed to the Prime Minister on Harrison's behalf. In 1773 Harrison was awarded £8,750, but the Board insisted this was a bounty, not the prize.

In 1772 James Cook had taken one of Harrison's 'sea clocks' with him on his second voyage. When he returned in 1774 he pronounced it completely satisfactory, having been able to make the first accurate charts of the South Sea Islands. Cook took the timepiece with him again on his third and final voyage.

Harrison died in 1776. The Board of Longitude was disbanded in 1828, and although the main prize was never actually awarded, Harrison had been the main winner with disbursements over time in effect totalling the amount of the prize money offered.

Harrison's first four sea clocks are preserved in working order today in the National Maritime Museum.

John Harrison.

THE BUCCANEER WITH AN ENQUIRING MIND

William Dampier was born in Somerset, England, in 1652. He was orphaned while a teenager and started his sea career apprenticed to a ship's captain on a voyage to the Newfoundland fisheries. He so hated the cold, however, that he made sure the rest of his travels were to the tropics, first as a sailor before the mast on an East Indiaman to Java.

When he returned he served in the Royal Navy for a time. He then worked as a sugar plantation manager in Jamaica, after which he found employment with the logwood cutters in Campeachy, Mexico. The dye of the logwood was highly prized for textiles but it was arduous work. The area was the nursery of English buccaneers at the time and Dampier found himself attracted to their free-wheeling lifestyle.

Much of his life at sea from then on was as a buccaneer. Dampier circumnavigated the globe three times, visiting all five continents and taking in regions of the world largely unknown to Europeans.

When not engaged in plunder he took careful notes of the places he visited – their geography, botany and zoology and the culture of the indigenous peoples. He carried his journal with him in a joint of bamboo sealed with wax at both ends. It was published in 1697 as *A New Voyage Around the World* and was followed by several other popular books. As a result Dampier was taken up by London society and he came to the notice of the British Admiralty. In 1699 he was sent on a voyage of discovery around Australia in HMS *Roebuck*. Unfortunately he lost the ship when it was wrecked at Ascension Island, which ruled out any further employment with the Royal Navy. He went back to buccaneering.

Future navigators benefited from Dampier's geographic surveys and observations, especially his 'Chart of the General and Coasting Winds in the Great South Ocean', 1729. This was the world's first integrated pattern of the direction and extent of the trade-wind systems and major currents around the earth.

Chapter 3.

The Sailors' WOODEN WORLD

The Sailors' WOODEN WORLD

Introduction

There was something very special about a sailing ship under full canvas, with nothing but the ocean winds and the skill of the mariner to carry her to the four corners of the world. At the height of the age of sail the man-of-war was the moon rocket of its day, a complex, self-contained community of 800 or more men. Day and night it could move faster than a man could run on land and was far taller than most buildings ashore. Its construction required the timber from 5,000 oak trees and it had nearly 2 hectares of sail and 40 km of rope and rigging. It could remain at sea for six months or more, carrying huge quantities of supplies including 110 metric tons of shot, 27 metric tons of meat and 40 metric tons of ship's biscuit.

It was a tough life for the common sailor. Not for nothing do we talk about iron men in wooden ships. But life at sea was often better than life ashore. A sailor got to see the world, he had guaranteed food and drink every day – and if he was very lucky there was prize money that could set him up for life. There was, too, a unique chance to make your way up in the world. In the rigidly stratified society of eighteenth-century Britain the Royal Navy offered virtually the only path for someone of low birth, but with talent and a bit of luck, to become a gentleman. After Admiral Nelson and Captain Hardy the two most important people in HMS *Victory* at the

Battle of Trafalgar were both originally common seamen: John Quilliam and John Pascoe.

During the last days of the era the clipper ships, the greyhounds of the sea, could even give a steamship a run for its money. *Cutty Sark,* the famous tea clipper preserved in Greenwich, demonstrated this in an incident with the crack P&O steamship *Britannia* on 25 July 1889. *Britannia*, doing around 15 knots, was overhauled by *Cutty Sark* making a good 17 knots. Robert Olivey, second officer on *Britannia*, watched the lights of the sailing ship overhauling his vessel with amazement and then wrote in *Britannia*'s log: 'Sailing ship overhauled and passed us!'

In harbour – and a riotous time is had on the mess deck.

ANIMALS COMING ABOARD

Many sailing ships carried a variety of pet animals to sea, and officers and crew alike found respite from a hard life in their companionship and affection. All kinds of creatures found their way aboard: birds, dogs, cats, guinea pigs – even tame monkeys.

Cats often slept in miniature hammocks, lovingly crafted by sailors from old pieces of canvas. One of the most famous ship's cats was Trim, the affectionate and intelligent companion to Matthew Flinders during his epic voyages of discovery from 1799 to 1804. Flinders called him 'the best and most illustrious of his race' and wrote a moving biographical tribute to the feline, which remained hidden in the archives of the National Maritime Museum in Greenwich for many years. In 1966 a bronze statue of Trim was installed in the Mitchell Library in Sydney, Australia.

Dogs were popular pets, too. When HMS *Salisbury*, flagship of Vice-Admiral John Campbell on the Newfoundland station from 1783 to 1785, received orders to return to England, the admiral gave permission for any person who pleased to take home a dog – 75 were embarked.

Cuthbert Collingwood, perhaps second only to Nelson as one of the great sea heroes of the age, was respected for his seamanship and courage, but a somewhat cool and aloof leader. His warmth and humour were reserved for his family at home in England, and for Bounce, his canine companion at sea for many years. When Collingwood became admiral, Bounce seemed aware of his master's new status. Collingwood wrote home to his wife: 'The consequential airs he gives himself since he became a right honourable dog are insufferable. He considers it beneath his dignity to play with commoners' dogs, and truly thinks that he does them grace when he condescends to lift up his leg against them. This, I think, is carrying the insolence of rank too far.'

When he died Collingwood was deeply saddened, writing in a letter to his family, 'Bounce is dead. I am afraid he fell overboard in the night. He is a great loss to me. I have few comforts but he was one, for he loved me. Everybody sorrows for him. He was wiser than a good many who hold their heads higher.'

Bounce hid below-decks when the guns were fired, but some dogs relished a good sea fight. In January 1799 Captain Lewis Mortlock of HMS *Wolverine* found himself outnumbered two to one; in a desperate hand-to-hand fight he and his crew repulsed a ferocious attack with the aid of his fearless Newfoundland dog.

A parrot aboard HMS *Hinde* in 1793 had learnt to imitate the calls of the boatswain's whistle. Sometimes the bird would pipe an order so accurately that the ship was thrown into temporary confusion. One day, when a party of ladies was being hoisted on deck from a boat, the parrot piped 'Let go' – with the inevitable disastrous results.

Captain, Spare That Pig

On occasion seamen made a special pet of one of the animals destined for the table. In the brig *Onyx* in the late 1820s the crew grew attached to a piglet that travelled with them from Portsmouth to the West Indies. When they learnt that the pig, by now grown, was about to be butchered, a group of seamen took the brave step of sending a deputation to the captain to plead for its life. 'You see, sir,' they told him, 'he is just like one of us; he knows us all and takes his grog daily like any Christian.' The porker was spared the cooking pot.

When it was clear that the mighty *Santissima Trinidad* would not survive the storm that followed the Battle of Trafalgar in 1805, every effort was made to save those on board. They were lowered with ropes from the stern and quarter gallery windows as boats from nearby English warships came to rescue them. The lieutenant of HMS *Ajax,* whose boat was the last to leave the scene, reported, 'Everything alive was taken out, down to the ship's cat.' He had put off from the starboard quarter when a cat ran out on the muzzle of one of the lower-deck guns and gave a plaintive miaow. The boat returned and took her in.

Trim, beloved feline sea companion of Matthew Flinders.

USEFUL STUFF, VINEGAR

 At sea this versatile fluid was kept in a barrel, holding 32 gallons. The chines were white to distinguish it from other contents such as lime juice, indicated by green chines.

Fresh water was always in very limited supply on board sailing ships. It was made available from the 'scuttled butt', a barrel which had a square piece sawn out of the widest part of its curved side so that no more than half a butt was available each day. In times of action, when the men worked up a sweat and got very thirsty, it was necessary to have some means of further restricting how much they could drink, and this was done by adding vinegar.

Burns were common injuries on the gun deck, and compresses of vinegar were often applied as treatment. It was favoured as a local disinfectant on wounds. The surgeon kept a gang-cask open at the ready when the ship went into action.

The acidic liquid was put to good use to swab down areas of the ship –

deck-head beams were given particular attention if fever was detected. An effective method of fumigating against cockroaches was panning vinegar, flashing a dish of it with gunpowder. In action, the guns were sponged out with a mixture of vinegar and seawater.

And in the galley the addition of vinegar to foods provided a welcome change from the fairly bland food that was a seaman's lot. Cabbage, for example, was pickled in salt and water, boiled and then seasoned with vinegar.

> BATTEN DOWN THE HATCHES – prepare for a dangerous situation. DERIVATION: in bad weather at sea it was important to secure the ship's deck openings, the hatches, against any sudden ingress of water. This was done by fastening protective canvas over the hatch cover with flat pieces of wood called battens.

𝒜 MINI UNITED NATIONS

Unlike today, there were no nationality or citizenship requirements for life in the Royal Navy in Nelson's day. Foreigners made up a surprising proportion of the navy then. The Napoleonic Wars generated an overwhelming need for seamen, up from 45,000 in peacetime to 145,000 at the height of the conflict. They had to be found from somewhere as there just weren't enough British nationals to go around.

Some foreigners did volunteer, but a significant number found themselves serving in His Majesty's ships against their will. Although it was illegal to press foreigners, this was often done from merchant vessels at sea, when there was little chance of redress for the unfortunate victims.

In the ethnic mix around the mess tables black seamen were not uncommon, finding in the lower deck of a man-of-war a world in which their skills as a sailor counted more than their colour.

Americans made up the biggest number of foreigners. In 1813 one report stated that 6,600 Americans had obtained discharges from the navy in 1811–12. Alleged high levels of impressment of Americans was one factor in the War of 1812, in which America, resentful of what it saw as Britain's high-handed actions at sea, declared war on Britain.

Sometimes, as the political map changed over the years, foreigners who signed on when their countries were neutral later found themselves transformed into the enemy.

In 1808 the captain of HMS *Implacable* recorded in the ship's books that 14 per cent of the men were non-British. He did not find this exceptional, reflecting that if anything it was a bit lower than in other ships he knew of. In King George's navy as a whole there were sailors from England, Ireland, Wales, the Isle of Man, Scotland, Shetland, Orkneys, Guernsey, Canada, Jamaica, Trinidad, St Domingo, St Kitts, Martinique, Santa Cruz, Bermuda, Sweden, Denmark, Prussia, Holland, Germany, Corsica, Sicily, Minorca, Ragusa, Brazil, Spain, Madeira, USA, West Indies and Portugal.

Even at the Battle of Trafalgar, where an all-British crew might have been expected, around 10 per cent were non-British. In fact there were 108 Frenchmen in the British fleet, four of whom were in *Victory*. Most of the best French seamen came from Brittany and Normandy, areas that had many Royalist sympathisers.

Spinning a yarn to messmates.

*W*ATCH YOUR HEAD!

It was almost impossible for an officer to stand upright in the wardroom in many men-of-war, and only those seated in areas without beams directly overhead could get to their feet with some semblance of dignity. In those ships with a pronounced 'tumble-home', steeply sloping sides, this was even more of a challenge.

One concession to this is that in the Royal Navy the Loyal Toast to the monarch is drunk seated. William IV, the 'sailor king', was sent to sea at the age of 13 and saw active service in America and the West Indies. He reputedly bumped his head so many times toasting his father that he vowed that when he became king no officer would suffer a similar fate.

Toasts

As well as the Loyal Toast, a number of others were popular in the wardroom:

Sunday:	'Absent friends'
Monday:	'Our ships at sea'
Tuesday:	'Our men'
Wednesday:	'Ourselves, as no one else is likely to concern themselves with our welfare'
Thursday:	'A bloody war or a sickly season'
Friday:	'A willing foe and sea room'
Saturday:	'Sweethearts and wives – may they never meet'

The Thursday toast is a reference to the opportunity for promotion via a dead man's shoes, in peacetime often the only way to get ahead.

'*A* RED CHECKED SHIRT AT THE GANGWAY'

To our modern sensitivities discipline at sea in the age of sail appears very harsh, but it has to be seen in the context of the times – ashore a person could be sentenced to death at the gallows for a minor misdemeanour.

The Articles of War provided the legal basis for discipline in the Royal Navy, but the severity of punishment varied greatly from ship to ship, depending on the captain. Admiralty regulations allowed a maximum of 12 lashes with the cat-o'-nine-tails, but this was often ignored on the grounds that the man had offended in several ways at once.

A captain was not limited to the formal offences as specified in the Articles of War. He could punish 'according to the laws and customs and in such cases used at sea', and the punishments meted out could include flogging, an admonishment, the stopping of grog or the disrating of a petty officer.

On punishment day, at six bells in the forenoon watch, the order was given, 'All hands to witness punishment.' The master-at-arms presented the offender to the captain, who questioned the man about his alleged offence and then delivered a verdict. The officer of the offender's division was asked if he had anything to say in mitigation. If this did not satisfy the captain he ordered the man's punishment. For a flogging the man was stripped to the waist and tied to a grating. The bosun's mate then extracted the cat-o'-nine-tails out of a baize bag. Some of the tougher seamen took pride in receiving 'a red checked shirt at the gangway' without crying out.

However, the captain's jurisdiction was limited; he did not have the power of life or death and could not order some of the more extreme punishments. The most serious crimes, such as mutiny, arson and cowardice, were dealt with by court martial, which had to consist of at least five and not more than 13 captains and admirals. If a sailor was sentenced to death by a court martial he was hanged, whereas an officer was shot. The last capital punishment carried out in the Royal Navy was the execution of John Dalliger in 1860 on board HMS *Leven*.

Flogging around the fleet was one of the punishments that could only be ordered by a court martial. It involved being rowed from ship to ship with the victim bound to a triangle of spars and receiving a set number of lashes while alongside each. Incredibly, some survived the ordeal, including William Mitchell (500 lashes), who went on to achieve a King's commission and eventually the rank of admiral. The terrible punishment of keel hauling, in which a man was dragged under the ship's keel to the other side, his flesh torn by barnacles in the process, was permitted in the Dutch navy, but never used in the Royal Navy.

A midshipman who committed a misdemeanour was usually mastheaded. This meant being sent to the cross-trees at the top of the mainmast. There he had to sit exposed to all weathers until he was allowed to return to the deck.

A number of punishments could be awarded by the junior officers or petty officers without the formality of trial by a captain. The most common were 'starting', which meant hitting the man on the back with a knotted rope's end; 'gagging', tying the mouth open with an iron bolt between the teeth; and 'spreadeagling', securing him with limbs outstretched up in the shrouds.

Some punishments were carried out by the men themselves, 'running the gauntlet' for theft, or being turned out of a mess for objectional behaviour.

The Royal Navy officially suspended flogging in 1879, and to this day it is still suspended, not abolished...

Mastheaded.

RUN THE GAUNTLET – attacked or threatened with attack, physically or metaphorically, from all sides.
DERIVATION: in the age of sail 'running the gauntlet' was a punishment for thievery which obliged the accused sailor to make his way between two rows of his shipmates, each of whom was armed with a knotted rope to beat him. The master at arms went in front of the unfortunate man walking backwards with a cutlass drawn to prevent him getting through too quickly.

THE BAND OF BROTHERS

Nelson used this phrase on a number of occasions. It is from Shakespeare's play *Henry V* – 'We few, we happy few, we band of brothers.'

Nelson's original Band of Brothers were all captains at the Battle of the Nile in 1798 and they were the élite of the navy. Fifteen in number, they had known Nelson for a number of years and there was a unique trust and understanding between them.

Not all of the Nile captains were equally close to Nelson; he had an inner circle that he consulted regularly, and they then conveyed the results of these meetings to the remainder. But this inner circle was not static. Of the original Nile captains only Thomas Hardy served in all of Nelson's later battles. Alexander Ball became governor of Malta, and Ralph Miller was killed in an accidental explosion at the siege of Acre.

Captain George Westcott was the only one of the celebrated band to die at the Nile. He was born of humble origins and left a widow and daughter. Nelson made a point of visiting them and presented Mrs Westcott with his own Nile medal saying, 'You will not value it less because Nelson has worn it.'

The phrase 'band of brothers' later came to mean any captains who were close to Nelson.

The Nile captains.

RIGHT GOOD STOCKHOLM TAR

 A true man-of-war's man was said to be:

> Begotten in the galley and born under a gun
> Every hair a rope yarn
> Every tooth a marline spike
> Every finger a fishhook
> And his blood right good Stockholm tar

The rich aroma of pine tar has long pervaded sailing ships. Its use as a preservative for wood and rigging dates back at least 600 years. Stockholm tar (sometimes known as Archangel tar) is the most valued and derives its name from the company which for many years had a monopoly on its production in Sweden.

International politics influenced supplies of tar. In the eighteenth century England was cut off from Scandinavian supplies by Russia's invasion of Sweden–Finland. By 1725 four-fifths of England's tar and pitch came from the American colonies. This changed again with the American Revolution.

Stockholm tar with its distinctive resinous tang was used by a sailor to dress his queue, his clubbed plait of hair – hence his familiar name of Jack Tar. Not to be confused with this, pitch from the tar lakes of Trinidad, and sometimes called asphaltum, was used for caulking, the process of waterproofing the seams between planks on deck.

Jack Tar carrying a marline spike, gang cask and handy-billy tackle.

PLENTY OF SCOPE – sufficient resources to carry out a task. DERIVATION: from the Greek *skopos*, meaning to mark or aim, in nautical parlance scope is the length of cable run out when a vessel rides to anchor to safely clear her neighbours.

FIRST, TAP OUT THE WEEVILS

An entry in the *Encyclopaedia Britannica* of 1773 reads: 'Sea-bisket is a sort of bread much dried by passing the oven twice to make it keep for sea service. For long voyages they bake it four times and prepare it six months before embarkation. It will hold good for a whole year.' Generally, these hardy forms of carbohydrate were produced using just flour and water, and were about one-third heavier than the flour from which they were made.

The ship's biscuit (also known as hard tack) has a long association with seafarers, going back to the days of ancient Egyptian sailors. They were also favoured by the Greeks and Romans. Large quantities of ship's biscuits were stored at the Deptford Naval Yard as early as 1513. Basic, durable and almost indestructible, they provided a reliable source of energy for seamen doing hard physical labour in all weathers. The ration of biscuit per sailor was 450 g a day. One biscuit, dated 1784, now exhibited in the National Maritime Museum at Greenwich, attests to their keeping powers.

A perennial problem with ship's biscuits was infestation with weevils. A number of variations of the recipe were tried to remedy this, including adding caraway seed, but the pesky bugs merely ignored the additional ingredient. Admiral Muir suggested the polite way to deal with weevils was to split the biscuits open with a stout knife and scrape the insects off the cut surface. The more usual way to deal with them was with a brisk tap on the surface of the table so the weevils came out of their own accord. Sailors liked to crack the biscuits by breaking them open in the crook of their elbows.

If the biscuit was poorly baked the outside would crumble away, leaving a hard, rigid centre. These were called reef nuts and were not discarded. Hungry midshipmen collected them and nibbled them during the day – hence the nickname of 'reefer' for the young gentlemen. And if they couldn't face them in daylight they saved them up and ate them in the dark.

Maggots, nicknamed 'bargemen', also infested biscuits. They were cold to the taste in the mouth. One naval wit said, 'Bread, it is well remarked, is the staff of life; but it is not quite so pleasant to find it life itself, and to have the power of locomotion.'

Towards the end of the eighteenth century naval ships of the line stored biscuit in a special bread room. The steward's assistant collected the daily ship's ration from there. Because of the flour dust he was called Jack in the Dust or Jack Dusty. At the height of their production, the large bakehouses at Portsmouth and Gosport and other facilities were manufacturing thousands of biscuits a day.

Bakeries began to be fitted in naval ships in the mid 1850s, enabling fresh bread to be made available for the duration of the voyage. There were still large stocks of biscuit in the naval victualling stores, however, which were not going to be allowed to go to waste, and they continued to be supplied for a number of years. Moreover, the navy has not let the custom fade away; stout ship's biscuits are still purchased by the Ministry of Defence for use in operational ration packs.

For the merchant marine, ship's biscuits were an essential part of the sea diet. In the port city of Liverpool they were known as Liverpool Pantiles, after a type of roofing tile, because of their shape and texture. In many merchant vessels biscuits, along with salt meat, remained standard provisions until the late 1950s.

Midshipman, by Rowlandson.

$\mathcal{A}$ MARVEL OF THE AGE

In Georgian times England's six Royal Dockyards were the biggest industrial enterprises in the world, the most important ones being at Portsmouth and Plymouth. During the Napoleonic Wars 15,000 men worked in these dockyards, including 5,000 shipwrights, one-third of the number of that profession in the whole country. All told there were over 25 different trades. The dockyards were huge tourist attractions, drawing people from every walk of life, from ordinary citizens to artists to foreign dignitaries, all wanting to see the sheer scale and diversity of activity at first hand. Even the future Queen Victoria was taken to Portsmouth dockyard at the age of 12 as part of her education.

The dockyard at Portsmouth covered 33 hectares. Inside the complex were vast piles of timber and ironwork stacked on the ground. The clang and roar of smithies and the stink of tanneries assaulted the senses. There was all manner of buildings including storehouses, mast and plank houses, seasoning sheds, saw pits, shops for carpenters and other skilled workers, rigging houses, rope-walks 400 m long and the famous block mills. The dockyard did not just build and repair ships; it boasted massive bakeries, salting houses for preserving meat, and breweries.

Cornering the Block Market

A ship of the line needed over 1,000 blocks, the wooden pulleys through which ropes were hauled to control the sails and for other operations. At the end of the eighteenth century the navy was purchasing 100,000 blocks a year, all made by hand. Marc Brunel (the father of Isambard Kingdom Brunel) mechanised this process, creating the world's first production factory in Portsmouth dockyard, and by 1807 the Portsmouth block mills were meeting the navy's entire requirements, 10 unskilled men producing as many as 110 skilled craftsmen had done before.

In the early 1800s one visitor to Portsmouth dockyard noted that the heat of the anchor-forge was so intense that the men who worked there had to be supplied with 5 litres of beer a day. He marvelled that this, together with wages of 29 shillings a week, sufficed to tempt 'these Cyclops to abridge their lives and live in this emblem of Tartarus for sixteen hours a day'.

Fittings of block strops.

*L*OBLOLLY BOYS

The term is somewhat of a misnomer – they were nearly always old seamen, no longer fit for normal ship duties. They acted as assistants to the surgeon, with varying degrees of expertise and compassion. *Loblolly* is an old English word; its first known use was in the sixteenth century. The term is derived from *lob*, meaning to bubble, and *lolly*, a regional word for broth, or a kind of gruel. Loblolly was adopted in the navy to describe semi-liquid food given to the sick.

Loblolly boys were found in both the US navy and the Royal Navy. In US naval regulations the rate first officially appeared in 1814 (although it had been in common use for many years before). Sick call was announced by the loblolly boy standing at the foremast banging a mortar with a pestle.

Aboard USS *Chesapeake* a black loblolly boy called William Brown was the only person who could sound a trumpet and was rated bugleman by Captain Lawrence. Unfortunately his musical skill was not attended by martial temperament. Brown was court-martialled for failing to sound 'Boarders away' when ordered to do so.

Around the middle of the nineteenth century the Royal Navy replaced the rate of loblolly boy with that of sick-berth attendant. In the US, likewise, the loblolly boy faded into history with the introduction of the rate of surgeon's steward.

SPIN A YARN – telling a story by stretching out the truth. DERIVATION: the many miles of rope aboard wooden ships needed regular repair and maintenance. Pieces of old rope were teased out to make spun yarn, which was used for this purpose. As the mariners bent to their task they swapped tales as they worked, embellishing them in the telling.

THE SWINGING BED OF THE SAILOR

When Columbus landed in the Bahamas in 1492 he found that the natives used nets of cotton stretched between two posts as beds. They called them '*hamacs*'. This was changed to '*hamaca*' by the Spanish. Hammocks in the British navy stem from the age of Drake, when they were widely adopted, and were still on issue until recent times.

Before the introduction of hammocks sailors slept on the deck. During rough weather they would be thrown about and were often injured. The hammock was a vast improvement as it wraps around the sailor like a cocoon, making it virtually impossible to fall out of; and it moves in concert with the motion of the ship, while gravity keeps it in line with the others.

Hammocks were slung fore and aft, each at a numbered peg so that the sleeper was always in the same place and could be found quickly if needed. The official allocation of hammock space was 36 cm per man, or 71 cm if the man was a petty officer. However, with the two-watch system half the crew was on deck at any one time, so each man had twice that, in effect as much space as someone sharing a double bed today.

By Nelson's time each man had two hammocks, to allow for cleaning. They were made of canvas 1.8 m by 0.9 m and in each was a mattress made from flock or rags, a blanket and a coverlet. Hammocks belonged to the Navy Board and the men either brought bedding with them or purchased it from the purser.

Each morning hammocks were taken down and lashed with seven marling hitches, representing the seven seas. They were carried topsides to be stowed and aired, where they were put in special netting at the side of the ship to act as protection from musket balls under enemy fire.

Hammocks could also serve as life preservers; one thrown to a man overboard could keep him afloat for 24 hours. If a seaman died at sea he was sewn into his hammock with one or two round shot at his feet – and the last stitch through his nose.

In Nelson's day each sailor had two hammocks.

Sometimes females were allowed to stay on board overnight when a ship was in harbour. The women could linger an extra hour in the hammocks, providing they could prove their gender by showing a hairless leg to the bosun's mates as they did their rounds.

During the late 1700s the British prison system used hammocks in their correctional facilities in order to save space. The hammocks were hung from a brass wall hook or ring on one wall and secured to an opposite wall in the same manner, or to the bars of the cell. However, prisoners soon discovered that the metal hooks could be used as weapons for escape, and the use of hammocks was abolished.

*M*AL DE MER

 The intended bride of the future Edward II set sail from Norway in 1290 but became seasick on the voyage. Although the ship made a stop at the Orkney Islands to allow her to recover, she died.

From ancient times ship handling and fighting has been affected by *mal de mer*, or seasickness. Martin Frobisher, in an attempt to counter its effects, took ginger along with him on his 1576 voyage to discover the Northwest Passage.

Nelson always suffered at the beginning of a voyage, and Sir John Franklin was never able to take charge of his ship until he had passed the Bay of Biscay. The current Prince of Wales, who himself served in the navy, has been known to try to lift a sufferer's spirits by joking, 'If you want a guaranteed cure for seasickness, take my advice and just lie under the nearest tree for an hour.'

The attitude of the Royal Navy has always been that seasickness is not a malady but something you just put up with – and you get on with your job. One rear admiral recently echoed this official lack of sympathy when he stated that the stabilisers fitted to today's modern warships are not to prevent seasickness, but for the protection of the sensitive electronic equipment on board.

Colour-coded Admirals

King Edward I appointed the first English admiral in 1297. He was William de Leyburn, given the splendid title of 'Admiral of the sea of the King of England'. The Royal Navy has had admirals since at least as far back as the sixteenth century. At the time of Elizabeth I the fleet had become so large that it was organised into three colour-coded squadrons: red for the admiral's, white for the vice-admiral's and blue for the rear admiral's.

Later, as the number of ships in the fleet grew further, and the three squadrons into which they were divided became larger, three admirals were allocated to each battle fleet (based on the line of battle) – a full admiral in command in the centre, a vice-admiral as his second in command taking the van (forward) and a rear admiral as third in command in the rear. These ranked in the order red, white and blue, and admirals took rank according to the colour of their squadron. Some officers were promoted rear admiral, but to no particular squadron. They were known colloquially as yellow admirals.

In 1864 the organisation of the British fleet into coloured squadrons was discarded. The red ensign was allocated to the merchant navy, the Royal Navy adopted the white ensign, and the blue ensign was used by the naval reserve and naval auxiliary vessels.

Elizabeth I (Armada Portrait).

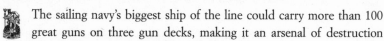

TOUCH AND GO – a precarious situation in which the slightest change could spell disaster. DERIVATION: sometimes a sailing vessel touched ground but then lifted off again quickly, thus avoiding disaster by a narrow margin.

$\mathcal{T}$HE BIG BANG

The sailing navy's biggest ship of the line could carry more than 100 great guns on three gun decks, making it an arsenal of destruction able to unleash as much firepower on the enemy as the mightiest fortress on land. The largest cannon weighed over three tons and could penetrate 2 feet of solid oak a mile away.

The production of cannon was a very skilled, time-consuming and expensive process – and there were never enough guns. To complicate matters, French and British guns had different calibres, so captured guns were of no use to the victor!

The Vergruggen family of Denmark established a gun foundry in Woolwich, England, which by 1780 had come to be regarded as the best in the world. Bronze guns (erroneously called brass cannon) were stronger and lighter, did not rust and could be polished to a high gleam, but with improvements in casting and the quality of iron they fell out of favour and during the French wars the typical navy gun was made of iron.

Count Rumford, the noted Georgian scientist, observing the extreme heat generated by the boring process during manufacture of cannon, developed theories of heat and energy that laid the basis for the modern science of thermodynamics.

British tactics were to try to get as close to the enemy ships as possible to shoot at the hull and sink the ship; most engagements were fought at less than 90 m. This made for a bloody encounter with murderous splinters of wood blasted from the timbers as well as the actual damage from the cannon balls.

Up to 20 men served each big gun during battle, led by the gun captain, a highly skilled sailor. Some of the gun crew had special duties such as boarding and sail-trimming and could be called away to these tasks even under enemy fire. A greatly feared hazard was an unsound cannon. Casting flaws could not be detected by the naked eye, and there was always the possibility that when fired a cannon could explode, with deadly consequences.

French 24-pdr run out.

THE FICTITIOUS PUSSER'S TALLIES

Life was hard for families of sailors who died at sea. Prize money was only distributed among survivors. The victim's shipmates would auction his possessions for a few coins to pass on to his widow, paying well over the odds for the items, but this would not put food in mouths for very long.

By an act of King George II each Royal Navy ship carried on the books one or two widows' men per 100 of her complement, depending on her circumstances. These men were purely fictitious and given 'pusser's tallies', imaginary names. Their pay went toward a fund for the relief of the families of warrant and commissioned officers who were killed in service. This practice lasted from 1760 to 1832.

However, even as early as the sixteenth century there was some formal help for injured sailors and their families. From 1590, all seamen in the Royal Navy made contributions of six pence per month from their wages to support the Chatham Chest, which paid pensions to injured seamen. Two men were largely responsible for setting up the fund, the heroes of the Armada campaign Sir John Hawkins and Sir Francis Drake.

Payments were on a sliding scale, £6 13*s.* 4*d.* per annum for the loss of a limb, £12 for blindness. In addition each claimant received a lump sum, equal to one year's entitlement. In effect this was the world's first occupational pension. However, during the 224 years that it existed there were a number of difficulties with meeting the payments, and from 1670 the government took over the administration of the system, for which responsibility was assumed by Greenwich Hospital in 1814.

The assets of the fund were kept in an actual chest at Chatham dockyard and secured by five locks, which opened to five separate keys held by five different officers, an expedient intended to prevent misappropriation of funds. The chest exists to this day and may be seen at the Chatham Historic Dockyard museum.

Greenwich Hospital

Greenwich Hospital was established by royal charter in 1694 and the first batch of wounded veterans, known as Greenwich pensioners, arrived there in 1705, where they spent the rest of their days in relative comfort. At its peak the hospital was sheltering and caring for 2,800 men. The able-bodied could wander in the streets of Greenwich or enjoy the green slopes of the park. And life there was not without its lighter moments. In 1796 there was a famous cricket match between the pensioners with one arm and those with one leg. The one-leggeds won. The charity also provided support for seamen's widows and education for their children.

A Greenwich Pensioner.

After each of the major naval battles of the 1790s a charitable subscription was started in the City of London to relieve the suffering of the wounded and bereaved. These were usually organised and managed by a committee of merchants at Lloyd's Coffee House, later to become the famous insurance market. The first of these funds was raised in 1794 after Lord Howe's victory over the French at the Glorious First of June. Howe donated his entire prize money from the battle.

Lloyd's Patriotic Fund, established in 1803, helped both wounded seamen and officers and dependants of seamen killed in action with cash sums. It was one of the first charitable trusts of this nature to be established in the world and continues to this day.

On the Way Up

 In the rigid social system of the eighteenth century, the Royal Navy offered virtually the only path for someone of low birth, but blessed with talent and luck, to become a gentleman.

During the 22 years of the bitter wars with France probably 600,000 seamen served their king and country. Of those, some 200 or more made the incredible transition from lower deck to officer rank. The odds were huge – 1 in 2,500 – but it did happen. And of those who made the quarterdeck possibly 16 became captains of their own ship and six achieved flag rank.

We know very little about this tiny handful of men. We do know that after Admiral Nelson and Captain Hardy the two most important people in HMS *Victory* at the Battle of Trafalgar were both from the lower deck: John Quilliam, first lieutenant, and John Pascoe, signal lieutenant.

Among the other heroic figures from before the mast was Provo Wallis, who joined the navy as an able seaman in 1795 and died in 1892 an admiral of the fleet. There was also James Clepham, a pressed man who was promoted to the quarterdeck in recognition of his role in a desperate cutting-out expedition in 1801. And Admiral Benbow, Captain Cook and Captain Bligh all rose above lowly origins...

Admiral Benbow.

A LOOSE CANNON – someone likely to cause trouble.
DERIVATION: cannon, which weighed up to three tons each, were mounted on wheels so that they could be quickly run in and out of gunports. They were secured with very strong ropes, but if they got loose in rough seas they would career all over the decks and in a heavy roll a cannon could get up enough momentum to smash through the side of the ship.

JOLLIES AND JOHNNIES

'Jollies' was the nickname for the trained bands of the city of London, a citizen army from whom the first marines were recruited in 1664 as sea-going soldiers, forming the Duke of Albany's Regiment of Foot. The origin of 'Jack/Johnny' for mariners is harder to trace, but Jack has long been used as a generic term for a working man.

Different Races

According to Captain Basil Hall, who served in the Napoleonic Wars, the difference between seamen and marines was absolute: 'No two races of men differ from one another more completely than the "Jollies" and the "Johnnies". The marines are enlisted for life, or for long periods as in the regular army. The sailors, on the contrary, when their ship is paid off are turned adrift and generally lose all they have learned of good order during the previous three or four years.'

Every warship with more than about ten guns had some kind of marine detachment. On board HMS *Victory*, for example, the marines included 146 officers and men. Marines, who could not be pressed, served as a professional military unit, both afloat and ashore. At sea they were employed to guard vital areas of the ship – the powder rooms, magazines, spirit room and the entrances to the officers' and admiral's quarters. They gave general assistance to seamen when unskilled heavy labour was required, such as hauling on ropes or turning the capstan, but were not obliged to go aloft. If there was any danger of mutiny, the marines had a paramount role in protecting the officers.

During battle they provided extra manpower to operate guns, and were useful for small-arms fire and close-quarters defence. They also participated in cutting-out expeditions against the enemy.

Seamen had no great inclination to mix with marines, a preference that was deliberately encouraged; they ate and slept separately. There was a certain amount of resentment among the officers of the two services, partly because the marines had a more impressive uniform, but also to do with the fact that mixed parties were generally put under the command of naval officers.

In 1802, largely at the instigation of John Jervis, Earl St Vincent, George III decreed that the soldiers of the sea henceforth would be known as the Royal Marines. Three years later in 1805 some 30,000 marines had been voted by Parliament, and Jervis said of them, 'If ever the hour of real danger should come to England, they will be found the country's sheet anchor.'

THE CALL OF NATURE

In sailing ships toilet arrangements were provided in the form of 'seats of easement', boxes with a round hole cut in the top. For sailors they were placed at the bow of the ship, at the aftermost extremities of the beakhead, a sensible position as this was essentially downwind and normal wave action would wash out the facility. The term 'heads' or 'head' originates from this. In British ships, heads is always in the plural to indicate both sides, as seamen were expected to use the lee side, down weather, so that waste would fall direct into the sea. In ships of some other nations they were referred to in the singular.

There were different arrangements for sailors and officers, depending on the size of the ship. Aboard HMS *Victory*, for example, over 650 men had to make do with two benches, each with two holes, placed on either side of the bowsprit. The deck here was open, in the form of a grating, to allow the free sluicing of waves across the area. Petty officers had a seat on either side of the bow. Two small enclosed spaces gave privacy for officers. The admiral, captain and senior officers had their own heads, aft, in the outer part of the great stern galleries.

Toilet paper was not invented in Britain until the late nineteenth century, but officers used newspaper or discarded paper. The seamen made do with scrap fibrous material such as oakum.

By the late eighteenth century there were even flushing toilets aboard some ships – those whose captains could afford them.

GONE BY THE BOARD – gone for good.

DERIVATION: the side of a ship is known as a board, and if a mast, for example, was carried away it was said to have gone by the board.

IN THEIR OWN WORDS

There aren't many letters from eighteenth-century seamen in existence – mainly because most Jack Tars were illiterate, but also because letters of ordinary people were not often saved for posterity.

The few that have survived offer poignant insights into those times. Here are excerpts from two. The first is from a pressed man in HMS *Tiger*, writing home to his wife after the capture of a Spanish port.

My dear Life:

When I left you, heaven knows it was with an aching heart to be hauled from you by a gang of ruffians but however I soon overcame that when I found that we were about to go in earnest to right my native country and found a parcel of impudent Spaniards... and God knows, my heart, I have longed for this for years to cut off some of their ears, and was in hopes I should have sent you one for a sample now. But our good admiral, God bless him, was too merciful. We have taken Porto Bello with such courage and bravery that I never saw before – and for my own part, my heart was raised to the clouds and I would have scaled the Moon had a Spaniard been there to come at him... My dear, I am well, getting money, wages secure, and all Revenge on my Enemies, fighting for my king and country.

The next is from a young man who visited a friend in his ship who had joined the navy previously.

I spent the evening with him very pleasantly, and the sailors of his mess, as is their manner in men-of-war, procured us plenty of wine and everything that could be got to make a stranger comfortable; when morning came and I should go ashore, I felt reluctant to part with my friend, and instead of doing so I volunteered to serve His Majesty...

THE BENEFITS OF CLARET

Officers often recorded their wine consumption in terms of bottles, rather than glasses. One of the Royal Navy's most colourful characters, Thomas Cochrane, recalled trying to avoid getting too drunk during his youthful years in the navy by pouring some of his wine down his sleeve. He was discovered and narrowly escaped the standard punishment of having to drink a whole bottle himself. French wine was popular, often from captures, and claret was said to 'assist the memory, give fluency to speech and animate the mind with real gaiety to enliven conversation'.

Sign Up, Lads

An eighteenth-century poster calling for volunteers to join one of His Majesty's ships bound for the North American station read:

Who would enter for a small craft whilst the *Leander*, the finest and fastest sailing frigate in the world, with a good spar deck overhead to keep you dry, warm and comfortable, and a lower deck like a barn where you may play at leap-frog after the hammocks are hung up, has room for one hundred active smart seamen and a dozen stout lads for royal yard men? This wacking double-banked frigate is fitting out... to be a flagship on the fine, healthy, full-bellied North American station, where you may get a bushel of potatoes for a shilling, a codfish for a biscuit, and a glass of boatswain's grog for twopence. The officers' cabins are building on the main deck on purpose to give every tar a double berth below. Lots of leave on shore! Dancing and fiddling on board! And 4 pounds of tobacco served every month! A few strapping fellows who would eat an enemy alive wanted for the Admiral's barge. Every good man is almost certain of being made a warrant officer, or getting a snug berth in the dockyard... God save the King, the *Leander* and a full-bellied station!

A CLEAN SLATE – a fresh start. DERIVATION: during a voyage all the current sailing orders were chalked up on a slate by a quartermaster, as instructed by the officer of the watch. Variations in the course to steer, the set of the sails and other important information were noted or amended. The slate was wiped clean at the beginning of a new watch or when the ship was safely at anchor in harbour.

JUST ONE NIGHT

On 19 March 1801 Captain Richard Keats assumed command of HMS *Superb*. For the next four years and five months, until he put her into dockyard hands for repair on 22 August 1805, he would spend only one night out of his ship. While this probably is a record, service in the Royal Navy often meant long periods of time away at sea: Nelson was on blockade duty for two years and three months without setting foot off HMS *Victory*, and Collingwood once kept at sea for 22 continuous months, never dropping anchor. After Nelson's death at Trafalgar Collingwood spent the next five years almost perpetually at sea. In 1809 he wrote to his wife, 'I shall very soon

Resolute devotion to duty.

enter my fiftieth year of service, and in that time I have almost forgot when I was on shore.' Worn out from tireless devotion to duty he died at sea the next year, four days after finally being recalled home.

ANCHORS AWEIGH!

The earliest anchors were just large stones attached by rope to the craft. They were held by friction and were inefficient. The break-through came when a wooden crossbar or stock set at right angles enabled the anchor to dig itself into the seabed, no matter which way it fell.

However, it is not the anchor itself that holds ships in fixed positions against a current but the weight of the anchor cable, which acts like a spring. Ideally, its length is between three and a half and five times the depth of water.

Eighteenth-century anchors were made from massive iron rods forged to form the shank and arms. These component parts were then welded together in a hammer forge. In those days, however, there was no means of checking welds, which meant that hidden defects could sometimes cause anchor arms to break off under severe strain.

In the largest wooden warships, in addition to two main anchors, called bowers, there were two sheet anchors which served as spares, a stream anchor which was lightweight and ideal for low tide, and two kedge anchors which were used for operations such as warping the ship (hauling her to a fixed point using large ship's ropes).

The Admiralty pattern anchor is the type most readily recognised as a typical sailing vessel anchor, reaching its peak in the nineteenth century. Curiously, devices of rank at all levels in the navy, from a seaman's rating badge to the flag of the Lord High Admiral and the Admiralty itself, feature the anchor fouled. This is an abomination to any seaman, an anchor entan-gled with its cable being more likely to drag. Equally curiously, the only one not being required to display it is the lowly able seaman.

Weighing anchor in a ship of the line was an extraordinarily complex operation involving up to 300 men. In HMS *Victory*, for example, each main anchor stood the height of two or three men and weighed about 4 metric tons, and each anchor cable itself weighed over 6 metric tons, making a massive dead lift of over 10 metric tons. This load had to be lifted manually, as there was no mechanised means of providing power. The anchor cable itself was about 60 cm in circumference; in order to heave on the cable and weigh anchor a smaller endless rope, the 'messenger', was seized to it and this was the one taken around the capstan.

Hovelling

The occupation of hovelling could earn a man a respectable living in the Downs, a favoured anchorage off Deal in Kent. When ships lost their anchor in a storm, hardy local mariners braved horrific sea conditions to carry out replacement anchors that they had previously salvaged from the seabed. The endangered ships had no choice other than to pay a good price.

THREE SHEETS TO THE WIND – intoxicated and staggering about. DERIVATION: sheets are lines used to control sails and each sail has its own set of sheets. If these were carried away or allowed to run free the sails flapped uncontrollably. This was bad enough, but if the sheets on all three masts came loose, the situation was out of control.

BACK FROM THE BRINK

Most sailors could not swim, preferring the thought of a quick end if they were swept overboard, rather than a slow, lingering death as they struggled on until exhaustion overtook them. But a ducking in Neptune's Realm did not automatically mean a death sentence – around one-third of sailors who went overboard were rescued. Before the development of modern resuscitation techniques a near-drowned person was often placed face down over a barrel, which was then rolled vigorously back and forth to drain the water from his lungs. A favourite restorative of the ship's surgeons was hot onion soup, which was believed to stimulate breathing. Other treatments included bleeding and forcing tobacco fumes into the victim.

So young ...

George III once asked a senior naval officer what was the proper starting age for a youngster intent on a sea career and was told: 'Fourteen is as late as so hardy a profession can be embraced with the smallest chance of success.' His son, the future William IV, was then sent off to sea shortly before his 14th birthday.

Some were even as young as 10, but most entered service at 12 or 13. The Royal Navy divided them into classes of 'boys', first, second or third class, depending on their age.

Horatio Nelson joined at the age of 12. As a boy he was known as Horace and in March 1771, then a frail-looking lad, he stepped down from the stagecoach near Chatham dock and made his way to HMS *Raisonnable*. He later recalled how nobody seemed to be expecting him and how he spent much of that day and night endlessly pacing the deck. It was a lonely and depressing introduction to the navy. His uncle Captain Suckling had agreed to take him on as a midshipman in his ship but had written in a letter to his father, 'What has poor Horace done, who is so weak, that he above all the rest should be sent to rough it out at sea...? But let him come; and the first time we go into action a cannon ball may knock off his head, and provide for him at once.'

One 11-year-old wrote home to his mother:

'Indeed we live on beef which has been 10 or 11 years in corn and on biscuit which makes your throat cold in eating it owing to the maggots which are very cold when you eat them, like blancmange being very fat indeed... I do like this life very much, but I cannot help laughing heartily when I think of sculling about the old cider tub in the pond and Mary-Anne capsizing into the water just by the mulberry bush... I hope I shall not learn to swear, and by God's assistance I shall not...'

Norwich Duff was a 12-year-old midshipman on board HMS *Mars*. After the Battle of Trafalgar he wrote home to his mother about the death of the captain. 'My Dear Mama, you cannot possibly imagine how unwilling I am to begin this melancholy letter... He died like a hero, having gallantly led his ship into action, and his memory will ever be dear to his king, his country and his friends.' The hero he referred to was his own father, who had been decapitated by a cannonball. His headless body covered by an ensign lay where it fell on deck until the end of the battle. Norwich Duff was not put off naval service after this, and eventually rose to the rank of admiral.

Boys as young as ten years old went to sea.

TO THE BITTER END – seeing something through relentlessly, to the last stroke of adverse fortune.
DERIVATION: if a crew lets all the cable run out while anchoring, the rope will come to its bitter (inner) end, the turn of the cable around the mooring bitts at the ship's bow. There is no more to let out.

*F*ROM LITTLE ACORNS MIGHTY OAKS GROW

The supply of timber came to be one of the main constraints of naval power during the Napoleonic Wars. To build a ship of the line like HMS *Victory* the timber from about 6,000 trees was required. Oak, prized for its strength and durability under exposure, was by far the most valuable timber, often accounting for 90 per cent of the timber in a ship's hull. The Wealden forests of Kent and Sussex were an important source. Later, oak was imported from Danzig, modern Gdansk.

In 1793 the cost of a 74-gun ship of the line was just under £50,000. Construction took several years. Curved or 'compass' oak, which could take up to 100 years to grow to size, was highly valued and was used for stern-posts, frames, knees, etc. This often came from isolated trees, deliberately constrained during their growth. Straight oak was used for beams, planking and strengtheners.

Concerned at the dwindling supply of timber, Admiral Collingwood decided to do something about it himself. He loved to walk the hills of his Northumberland estate with his dog and would always start off with a handful of acorns in his pocket; whenever he found a good place for an oak tree to grow he would press a few into the soil.

Building England's wooden walls required vast quantities of timber.

JANE TAR

Many sailors believed that to have a woman on board would bring bad luck to the ship in the form of a terrible storm that would destroy the vessel and all in her. Female mariners were not common in the age of sail, but life at sea was not completely a male preserve.

Pirate lore tells of women sea captains such as the fearless Irish pirate Grace O'Malley and French noblewoman Jane de Belleville, who sought to avenge her husband's death by ravaging the coast of Normandy. Some women went to sea disguised as men. Hannah Snell enlisted in the marines and for over five years managed to conceal her true sex. During that time she took part in the attack on Pondicherry in India and was wounded in battle. Back in England she finally revealed her secret and became somewhat of a celebrity.

One person's true sexual identity could not help but be discovered at the Battle of Trafalgar when British sailors pulled a naked woman out of the water. This was 'Jeanette', who had disguised herself as a seaman when the French fleet sailed from Cadiz because she could not bear to be parted from her sailor husband. Although she initially feared he had been killed, the couple were later reunited.

There were of course women who came on board when the ship was at anchor, a mixture of prostitutes and those who claimed a more established relationship. Some wives of standing officers went to sea; they assisted with the care of the sick and wounded and even acted as powder monkeys during battle.

John Nichols, a seaman aboard HMS *Goliath*, wrote of the women on board ships during the Battle of the Nile, recording that some were wounded, and one died. During the Glorious First of June in 1794 Mrs Daniel McKenzie of HMS *Tremendous* went into labour and delivered her son in the bread room. The infant was named Daniel Tremendous McKenzie. He was awarded the naval General Service Medal, his rating being recorded as 'baby'.

Ann Hopping was born in Devon in 1769 and served as seamstress to Captain Saumarez in *Orion*. Her husband Edward was on board and both of them were present at the Battle of St Vincent and the Battle of the Nile. In 1847 the British government awarded a special medal to all living survivors of the major battles fought between 1793 and 1840. Ann and several other women applied and were originally approved, but later refused on the basis that 'there were many women in the fleet equally useful and it would leave the army exposed to innumerable applications of the same nature'. Ann Hopping remained at sea until her husband died. She remarried and lived to the age of 96 and was buried in Exmouth – in the same church grave-yard as Nelson's wife Fanny.

IRISH HORSE AND DOG'S BODY

The daily diet of a seaman serving in one of Henry VIII's ships was virtually unchanged for his descendants serving in Nelson's navy 300 years later. It consisted largely of ship's biscuits and salted meat, with some cheese, peas, oatmeal, sugar and butter. Although adequate in terms of calories (up to 5,000 per day) for hard work at sea, the food was often of poor quality and the diet lacking in vitamins and minerals.

From Drake's day onwards the crew ate in groups of six to eight called messes. Each man would take his turn as mess cook and collect the day's rations from the purser's steward in readiness for the noon meal. The prepared food, which varied with the skill and interest of the man on duty, was taken to the galley to be cooked (each mess marked their food with a tag). The mess cook was responsible for washing up the utensils and generally cleaning the eating area after the meal. He was entitled to an extra tot of rum for his trouble.

The mess cook carved and served the meal. To ensure fairness, one of the other men was blindfolded, a portion of the meat was carved, the blindfolded man called out a name and the portion went to that man and so on, until it was served. However, this system was not always followed, and younger mess members were sometimes bullied and deprived of the best victuals by older men.

The ship's cook was no trained culinary master. Usually a disabled seaman, often having suffered an amputation, his main role was to ensure the galley was run efficiently and that the boiling coppers were cleaned daily.

Sailors had their own names for certain items of their diet:

Cornish duck	pilchards
Dog's body	pigs' trotters with pease
Crowdy	watery porridge
German duck	boiled sheep's head
Lobscouse	stew made with pounded biscuits
Irish horse	salt beef

Canned meat and vegetables was first tried out in the Channel Fleet in 1813. It became known as bully beef because it was adapted from the French recipe for *boeuf bouilli* (boiled beef). In 1866 the Victualling Office itself began to manufacture it. Unfortunately, the very next year a famous prostitute named Fanny Adams was murdered and her body cut up into small pieces. The word went around among seamen that what the authorities were providing was Sweet Fanny Adams.

Ship's cook by Rowlandson.

LIFELINE – a source of salvation in a crisis.

DERIVATION: in foul weather, ropes were rigged fore and aft along the deck of a ship to provide a secure handhold for a sailor to grip to prevent him from being washed overboard. If conditions turned extremely nasty a sailor would grab the line and wrap it around his arm for extra security – then hang on for dear life!

RUMBUSTION

 Since the early days of sailing ships the most readily available liquids to take on voyages were water and beer, both of which could only be stored for a short time before they became unpalatable.

Vice-Admiral William Penn's fleet conquered Jamaica in 1655, and it was here that rum, or rumbustion, was first issued on board ships of the Royal Navy. Rum was also called rumbullion, kill devil, Barbados waters and red-eye.

Rum has the advantage of keeping well, even improving with age. When abroad captains of ships were allowed to replace beer with fortified wine, sometimes brandy, but neither was available in the West Indies. Rum was, however, and it became a popular drink ration in this part of the world, even though the Victualling Board back in England had not officially sanctioned its use.

From 1655 well into the eighteenth century the issue of rum very much depended on individual captains. In 1731 it was officially decreed that if beer was not available then each man was entitled, daily, to a pint of wine or half a pint of rum or other spirits.

In 1740 Admiral Vernon (nicknamed Old Grogram because of the boat cloak he wore made of that material) ordered that the rum issue be diluted 1:4, and thereafter the drink was called grog. He talked of 'the swinish vice of drunkenness'.

By 1793 the dilution was usually 1:3. From Vernon's day until the end of the Napoleonic Wars two issues of grog per day remained the custom whenever beer was unavailable. But the use of rum gradually became more widespread, as did the issuing ritual. The ship's fiddler played 'Nancy Dawson', the signal for the mess cooks to repair to the rum tub to draw rations for their messmates. This was always done in the open air because of the combustible nature of rum.

Rum was a currency aboard ship, with special terms for various amounts of the spirit. Gulpers meant one swallow, but as much as you could drain in one go; sippers, a more genteel amount as suggested by the name; and sandy bottoms, the entire tot.

The American Navy ended the rum ration on 1 September 1862, but the practice continued in the Royal Navy for over a century. Friday 31 July 1970 saw the last issue and became known as Black Tot Day.

The First Sea Lord issued this message to the Royal Navy:

> Most farewell messages try
> To jerk a tear from the eye
> But I say to you lot
> Very sad about tot
> But thank you, good luck and good-bye.

ADMIRAL VERNON.

'Old Grogram' gave his name to the sailors' favourite tipple.

SET UP FOR LIFE

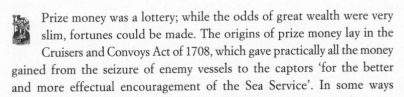

Prize money was a lottery; while the odds of great wealth were very slim, fortunes could be made. The origins of prize money lay in the Cruisers and Convoys Act of 1708, which gave practically all the money gained from the seizure of enemy vessels to the captors 'for the better and more effectual encouragement of the Sea Service'. In some ways prize money was unfair – all ships within sight when the capture took place were entitled to equal shares. And the admiral under whose orders the ship sailed was entitled to a share even if he was nowhere in the vicinity.

The following distribution scheme was used for much of the Napoleonic Wars, the heyday of prize warfare:

One-eighth went to each of these groups – flag officer; the captains of marines, lieutenants, masters, surgeons; lieutenants of marines, secretary to the flag officer, principal warrant officers, chaplains; midshipmen, inferior warrant officers, principal warrant officers' mates, marine sergeants. Two-eighths went to each of these groups – captains; the rest. The latter included all the seamen, many hundreds of men.

The taking of prizes could be very lucrative. The record haul came from the capture of the treasure-carrying Spanish vessel *Hermione* in 1762 by two British frigates. When the pay of a seaman was less than a shilling a day, the prize money in this instance to each seaman of £485 (nearly 35 years' salary for a few hours' work in the afternoon) promised to set them up for life – if they didn't spend the proceeds on too many rollicking celebrations ashore. Their share pales into insignificance, however, beside what the two captains responsible were awarded: £65,000 each, or over £8,000,000 in today's money. The treasure was conveyed from Portsmouth to the Tower of London in 20 wagons and was greeted in the capital by a troop of light dragoons, a band and joyous spectators.

After taking a number of rich prizes Captain Thomas Cochrane in HMS *Pallas* famously sailed into Plymouth with three five-foot-high gold candlesticks at the masthead. Among the other naval officers who amassed enormous sums were Hyde Parker, who realised £200,000 when he was in command in the West Indies, and Peter Rainier and Edward Pellew, who accrued around £300,000 each during their careers.

It was usually only frigates that took prizes. Ships of the line were too ponderous to be able to capture the smaller ships that carried treasure. However, 'gun money' and 'head money' was paid on larger captures, which went some way to compensate.

Nelson did not fare well with prize money. This was not so much bad luck as the irony that, largely due to his genius, Britain achieved mastery of the sea – and few enemy ships dared to sail.

The distribution of prize money to crews of ships involved persisted in the Royal Navy until 1918.

The magnificent Shugborough Hall in Staffordshire, built with the fortune Admiral Anson amassed from prize money.

THE SILENT SERVICE

When Napoleon surrendered to HMS *Bellerophon* shortly after the Battle of Waterloo he remarked, as the ship was getting under weigh, 'Your method of performing this evolution is quite different to the French. What I admire most in your ship is the extreme silence and orderly conduct of your men. On board a French ship everyone calls and gives orders and they gabble like so many geese.' Then, before he left *Bellerophon*, he said, 'There has been less noise in this ship, where there are 600 men, during the whole time I have been in her than there was on board the *Spervier* [a French frigate] with only 100 men in the passage from Isle d'Aix to Basque Roads.'

Later, on the voyage to the South Atlantic, Napoleon was also struck by the way the crew of HMS *Northumberland*, taking him to exile in St Helena, performed their duties in a similar manner. This was not unusual, however. Work in the Royal Navy was generally performed in silence.

Chapter 4.

Briny

BELIEFS & SUPERSTITIONS

Briny BELIEFS & SUPERSTITIONS

Introduction

Misconceptions about the sea and mariners abound across history. Many endure to this day, such as the myth of the ruthlessness of the press gangs. Although often rough-handed, they were regulated as to whom they could take and certainly did not have carte blanche to drag innocent young men off to sea. Fanciful accounts of the life of that great sea hero Horatio Nelson also enjoy popular currency. His body was not pickled in rum after his death at Trafalgar, nor were his last words 'Kiss me, Hardy'.

It is true, however, that those who follow the sea have always been among the most superstitious people on earth. Some notions, including those about the weather such as 'when the rain's before the wind, strike your tops'ls, reef your main', often have more than an element of truth in them. One above all, the fabled Fiddler's Green, the sailors' Elysium of perpetually flowing rum casks and willing wenches, no doubt gave comfort to sailors – should they die at sea they would not end as food for fishes but go to a better place. Superstitions, meanwhile, for example the belief that setting sail on a Friday brings bad luck, may have little to back them up, but are still held today.

Life at sea goes at its own pace, and a good yarn-spinner was always a popular member of any crew. Tales such as the legend of Cornish lass Sarah Polgrain, who came back from the grave to enforce her seaman lover's promise of marriage, would be embroidered at every telling – and the more entertaining the better! Lurid details of encounters with mermaids and denizens of the deep held a salty audience spellbound – and guaranteed that the story-teller's pot of grog seldom ran dry.

Sea serpent, from a sixteenth-century book on Nordic folklore.

*I*F YOU NEED ME, YOU KNOW WHAT TO DO

There are legends a-plenty about the Devon-born Elizabethan sea hero Francis Drake. It is said that when he supplied the city of Plymouth with water from the high moor nearby he muttered magic words over a stream and the leat followed him back to the gates of the city. He once whittled on a stick in the harbour and as each shaving fell into the water it was transformed into a fireship which wreaked havoc among the Spanish Armada.

Even Drake's love life had a supernatural twist. While he was harrying Hispanic ships the lady betrothed to him, fearing him dead, gave her hand to another. As the wedding party entered the church a cannonball fell just short of the building, like a shot across the bows of the bridegroom warning him that Drake was very much alive. Elizabeth Sydenham, the shocked bride, called off the wedding and in due course became Drake's wife.

On occasion Drake even joins King Arthur to lead the Whist Hunt across the land. Accompanied by spectral hounds with eyes of fire, he rides in a black carriage pulled by four headless horses. They search for no mundane quarry such as fox or deer, but the souls of unbaptised babies.

A more benign legend, that of Drake's Drum, was celebrated in a famous poem by Henry Newbolt:

Take my drum to England, hang it by the shore
Strike it when your powder's runnin' low
If the Dons sight Devon, I'll quit the port o' Heaven
An' drum them up the Channel as we drummed them long ago.

On his voyages around the world Drake carried with him a snare drum emblazoned with his coat of arms. When he lay dying off the coast of Panama in 1596 he expressed the wish that the drum be taken back to Devon, promising that if anyone beat on it when England was in danger he would return and lead her to victory. It is believed that Drake has returned twice, reincarnated once as Admiral Robert Blake and then as Admiral Horatio Nelson.

The drum has been known to sound without the help of human hands when significant national events take place, and there are reports that it was heard at the beginning and end of the First World War.

Drake's Drum now has pride of place at the Buckland Abbey Maritime Museum in Devon, England.

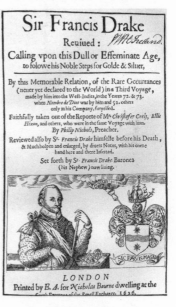

Drake's biography, 1626.

$\mathcal{P}$OLLYWOGS AND BADGER BEARS

Crossing the Line is a ceremony still performed by both naval and merchant ships to celebrate passing through the equator in a north–south direction. Today's version, however, is a good deal less rowdy than in the Golden Age of Sail. In the early days, the ceremony was a test for the novices on board to see if they could endure the hardships of life at sea. One account from 1708 tells of sailors being hoisted up on the yard and then ducked into the sea up to 12 times. This evolved into a less hazardous version involving a large canvas bath filled with seawater on deck, with a plank across it that could be suddenly withdrawn.

Before the ship actually crossed the line an emissary from the court of

King Neptune appeared on board. He brought a message for the captain announcing when the king would be arriving and presenting a list of those who were to appear before him.

On the actual day, the pollywogs, those who had not yet obtained their freedom from Neptune, were confined below decks, to be released one by one. King Neptune arrived accompanied by his wife Queen Aphrodite, together with an evil-looking barber, a grim-faced surgeon, fierce-looking guards and various nymphs and badger bears. After parading round the ship, the group convened a court on a platform beside the bath filled with seawater. King Neptune summoned the pollywogs in turn. The barber besmeared their faces with a foul mixture of tar and grease and then scraped it off with a hoop iron 'razor'. The surgeon administered 'medicine' and then these unfortunates were tipped into the bath for a good ducking.

A ship might remain for weeks in the belt of calm that lies close to the equator known as the doldrums. While in this region all aboard suffered from enervating conditions and longed for a breeze. Departure from the doldrums was therefore a time for thanksgiving.

King Neptune, in Ovid's Metamorphoses.

MAKING HEADWAY – progress of a general nature, sometimes hard won. DERIVATION: at sea, headway is the ship's forward movement through the water. Sometimes considerable effort was involved to achieve this, as when a ship tried to tack in a light breeze. The manoeuvre might have to be repeated several times before the sails filled and the cry was heard, 'She's making headway.'

PREST OR PRESSED?

During the desperate struggle with France from 1793 to 1815 the Royal Navy never had as many men as it needed. At the height of the conflict its authorised strength was up from 45,000 to 145,000. There were a number of ways the navy could man its ships – volunteers, quotas (compelling local authorities to supply a given number of men) and the press gang. The belief persists today that the navy's seamen consisted almost exclusively of pressed men, taken against their will and subjected to a harsh life at sea, condemning their wives and children to lives of poverty, but this is not so.

The press gang *was* universally loathed, but ordinary folk were generally not at risk. Legally, only those 'who used the sea', i.e. experienced mariners, could be pressed. There were some within this category, such as whalers and apprentices, who were issued with a 'protection' and were exempt, although in particular periods of manning crisis a 'hot press' occurred and these protections were ignored.

One reason for the myth of the press gang's impact comes down to two words, which in the course of time came to be spelt alike. A 'prest' man is a sailor who has received a 'prest', a sum of money in advance as an inducement to join the service. A 'pressed' man is one who has been taken by force. It is likely that less than half of the navy's seamen were actually pressed; the majority of them were volunteers.

However, there were abuses of the system and some gangs took men and boys with no previous experience of the sea. The Impress Service maintained gangs in various ports around Britain, organised into 32 districts each commanded by a naval captain. A press gang was usually led by a lieutenant, who bore a warrant signed by the Lords of the Admiralty, and consisted of about ten men.

When they got word that the press was about, sailors often came up with ingenious ways to escape capture, going to ground in the country or disguising themselves as females. A problem with the latter, however, was that their rolling gait and the tar on their hands often gave the game away.

Sometimes the seaports would rebel en masse and pitched battles between the townsfolk and press gangs ensued. Such was the unpopularity of the press that in December 1811 a near riot freed a suspected murderer from police custody as the mob mistakenly believed he was being pressed.

The Royal Navy is often called 'the Andrew', from Andrew Miller, a press-gang officer who was so efficient, ruthless and zealous in recruiting seamen that it was alleged he owned the navy.

Eighteenth-century caricature of a press gang at work.

ENTERING NEPTUNE'S REALM

When the first vessels took to the water a number of customs developed that were designed to appease the gods of the sea. Some involved human sacrifice; the Norse Vikings launched their warships over live prisoners tied to the launch-ways so their blood was carried into the sea.

In the Golden Age of Sail it was important to follow certain traditions to ensure good fortune for a ship and all who sailed in her. One of these was the custom of leaving coins under the step of a mast at the time the vessel was being built. This came down from the Roman tradition of placing a coin in the mouth of a dead person to pay the underworld ferryman Charon to transport him across the River Styx to Hades. If a ship met a mishap at sea the coins would ensure that the fares of the hands were paid.

When an English ship was launched a toast was drunk to her prosperity out of a silver cup, which was afterwards thrown overboard. In the late seventeenth century this was felt to be too extravagant and the practice of breaking a bottle over the ship began, performed either by a royal personage or a dockyard commissioner. In 1811 the Prince Regent introduced the custom of ladies performing the ceremony. However, one lady's aim was so poor that the bottle hit and injured a spectator, who sued. As a consequence the Admiralty decreed that henceforth the launching bottle should be secured by a lanyard to the bows.

Bless This Ship

French ship christenings in the eighteenth and early nineteenth centuries were accompanied by rites resembling marriage and baptismal ceremonies. A godfather for the new ship presented a godmother with a bouquet of flowers as both said the ship's name. No bottle was broken over the ship, but a priest blessed it with holy water.

Tradition has it that water was used in the first two attempts to launch the iconic USS *Constitution* ('Old Ironsides'), but she would not budge. It took a bottle of fine Madeira from the cellar of the Honorable Thomas Russell, a leading Boston merchant, to entice her to enter Neptune's Realm.

Charon, ferryman of the underworld.

WHEN A SAILOR TOPPED HIS BOOM

Sailors had a number of colourful expressions for death at sea, mostly involving nautical terms. Some sails need a long spar, or boom, to spread their foot. When the boom is topped, the vessel is ready to start the voyage. Sailors adopted the expression 'to top your boom' to refer to the journey to the afterlife, from which there was no return. Other salty euphemisms for dying were to 'cut your painter', 'slip your cable', 'cross the bar' and 'go aloft'.

A mariner might talk about meeting Davy Jones, the spirit of the deep. Davy Jones was thought to be in all storms and was sometimes seen as being of huge height, with three rows of sharp teeth in an enormous mouth, and emitting blue flames through his nostrils. The origin of this name is uncertain. It may be a corruption of 'Duffy Jonah', a West Indian sailors' name for the devil. Another explanation is that Davy derives from St David, the saint often invoked by Welsh sailors, and Jones comes from Jonah, the biblical figure swallowed by a whale. Some claim that Davy Jones was a London pub owner who kept drugged ale in a special cupboard and served it to the unwary, who were thus shanghaied – sent stupefied off to sea.

Davy Jones' Locker was the bottom of the sea, a sort of repository for everything that went overboard, from rigging to men. Sailors used to say, 'Nothing is lost, for you know where it is.'

Then there was Fiddler's Green, a mythical Elysium waiting for shellbacks, those who had been at sea for so long that barnacles grew on their backs, when they slipped their cable and went to their rest. In this paradise, populated by countless willing ladies, equipped with rum casks that never emptied, it was always a fair wind and flying fish weather. To get to Fiddler's Green the shell-back became a gull and then flew to the South Pole, where the entrance awaited him in the form of an open hatch.

Sailors did not like molesting sea birds, as they were thought to be the spirits of dead sailors who had not yet found their way to Fiddler's Green.

Unless the ship was very close to land, burial was at sea for most sailors. The body was sewn up in the man's hammock and weighted with a cannonball. At the last minute, a stitch through the nose confirmed that he was really dead! It became customary for the man who performed this task to claim a guinea a body. The French, however, brought their slain sailors home buried in the ship ballast so that they could be given Catholic rites.

Jack Tar was very uneasy about having a corpse on board ship, believing it would attract bad luck. If a corpse was carried on board there were some things that could be done to minimise the impact: it must always lie athwart the vessel, never end on, and when the home port was reached it must leave the ship before any member of the crew.

Yards a-cockbill indicated that the ship's captain had died.

CUT AND RUN – make off without warning.
DERIVATION: if the enemy suddenly came on a ship when she was at anchor, or if a sudden storm threatened to force her on to a lee shore, the captain would order the crew to cut the anchor cable and run downwind to escape.

FRIDAY SAIL, FRIDAY FAIL

For a sailor the day of his ship's departure was important. Wednesday was the best day of the week to begin and end a voyage – probably because the name derives from Woden's Day, the Anglo–Saxon god Woden being the chief protector of mariners. Friday, however, was to be avoided at all cost, an injunction that holds to this day. The Temptation and Banishment from the Garden of Eden, the Flood and the Crucifixion were all believed to have occurred on a Friday. Exceptionally, Spanish sailors favour Friday, as this was the day on which Columbus began his great voyages.

One admiral, a friend of Nelson's, once remarked: 'Why, I was once fool enough to believe that it was all nonsense, and I did once cruise, sail on a Friday, much to the annoyance of the men. The consequence was that I run my ship aground, and nearly lost her... nothing shall induce me to sail on a Friday again!'

*D*AMNED TO CEASELESS WANDERING

 The ghost ship is one of the most pervasive legends of the sea, and there is none more famous than *The Flying Dutchman*.

In the early eighteenth century a ship called *The Flying Dutchman* under Captain Vanderdecken set sail from Holland for the Cape of Good Hope. Then, according to nautical folklore, a great storm arose and the captain scoffed at the tempest and blasphemed. Suddenly a cloud opened up and a celestial figure descended on the deck. The captain fired a gun at this apparition, which put a terrible curse on him – to wander the oceans ceaselessly with neither rest nor fine weather, the sight of his ship bringing misfortune to all who see it.

It is said that the skipper of *The Flying Dutchman* on occasion personally visits passing ships. Sometimes he sends letters on board and if the captain reads them he is lost; he goes mad and his ship dances in the air, then pitches violently before sinking. Vanderdecken also leads ships on to rocks, turns wine into vinegar and rots food aboard.

The Flying Dutchman is a master of disguise, changing six times a day so as not to be recognised. Sometimes it is a heavy Dutch vessel, at other times a light corsair.

There were a number of reported sightings of *The Flying Dutchman* in the eighteenth and nineteenth centuries. One account, written in 1835, reads:

> Suddenly the second officer, a fine Marseilles sailor who had been the foremost in the cabin in laughing at and ridiculing the story of *The Flying Dutchman*, ascended the rigging and cried: '*Voilà le Hollandais Volant!*' The captain sent for his night glass and observed, 'It is very strange but there is a ship bearing down on us with all sail set, while we scarcely show a pocket-handkerchief to the breeze.'

Another report, made in July 1881 in HMS *Bacchante*, cruising in the Pacific, stated:

> At 4 a.m. *The Flying Dutchman* crossed our bows. A strange red light as of a phantom ship all aglow, in the midst of which light the masts, spars and sails of an old-fashioned brig 180 m distant stood out in strong relief as she came up. The look-out man on the forecastle reported her as close on the port bow, where the officer of the watch from the bridge clearly saw her, as did the quarterdeck midshipman, who was sent forward at once to the forecastle; but on arriving there no vestige nor any sign whatever of any material ship was to be seen

either near or right away to the horizon, the night being clear and the sea calm.

Sightings continued to occur past the age of sail. During the Second World War the German U-boat fleet commander Admiral Karl Dönitz reported that his crew told him they had seen the *The Flying Dutchman* on their tours of duty east of Suez.

The theme of *The Flying Dutchman* has inspired novelists, poets and composers – Marryat, Scott and Wagner among them. In modern times the legend was adapted into the *Pirates of the Caribbean* films.

> BY AND LARGE – in general. DERIVATION: a ship that performs well under most sailing conditions goes smartly into or 'by' the wind and also does not disappoint with a following wind or when 'going large'.

*T*HE *SHIPPE SWALLOWER*

The ancient town of Deal in Kent lies on the shore of the English Channel. Around 10 km out to sea lie the notorious Goodwin Sands, an uneven underwater platform of limestone, some 18 km long by 6.5 km across, over which many tons of shifting sands constantly flow. More than 2,000 ships have been wrecked there. At high tide the sands are covered by just 4 m of water. Some parts are treacherous quicksands which can swallow up whole vessels.

According to legend the sands were once a fertile, low-lying island called Lomea owned by Godwin, Earl of Wessex, after whom they are named. The land was later given to St Augustine's Abbey in Canterbury, but the abbot failed to maintain the retaining walls and the sea reclaimed the area. The Goodwin Sands quickly developed a sinister and feared reputation as 'the shippe swallower'.

In Shakespeare's *The Merchant of Venice*, Antonio has 'a ship of rich lading wracked on the narrow seas; the Goodwins, I think they call the place; a very dangerous flat and fatal, where the carcasses of many a tall ship lie buried.' Herman Melville mentions the sands in *Moby Dick*, as do R.M. Ballantyne, the Scottish writer, and the poets W.H. Auden and G.K. Chesterton.

Local stories tell of vessels claimed by the sands sometimes reappearing on the anniversary of their disasters. On 13 February 1748 Captain Reed aboard *Lady Lovibond* was toasting his recent marriage. His new wife and her mother, along with wedding guests, had joined him for a voyage to Portugal. However, First Mate John Rivers was consumed with jealousy at the match and after murdering the helmsman turned the ship into the sands. The bridal party below was too preoccupied to notice the change in direction until it was too late. On a number of occasions, in multiples of 50 years to the day, *Lady Lovibond* has been seen again and the sound of female voices has been heard coming from below deck.

Another sighting dates from the Spanish Armada. On board one of the galleons the Spanish captain prepared to surrender. One of his junior officers, rather than see the ship given to the English, turned on his captain and killed him and was then cut down himself. General fighting broke out among the other officers and the ship caught fire. Aflame from stem to stern, she was driven on to the Goodwin Sands, where she broke up and the crew perished.

Over 100 years later, in the Great Storm of 1703, four Royal Navy frigates, *Mary*, *Northumberland*, *Restoration* and *Stirling Castle*, all went to their doom on the Goodwins and hundreds lost their lives. A survivor from *Mary* reported: 'A great warship of Drake's day, her sails tattered, burning from fore to aft and her guns firing served by demented seamen bore down on us, sailed right through our ship and finally disappeared before our eyes into the depths of the sands.'

On 28 November 1753 the captain of an East India clipper inward bound for London saw the spectre of *Northumberland*. He recorded in his log that he watched the phantom ship go to her doom a second time on the sands. Some of the men aboard *Northumberland* leapt into the sea but made no splash as they entered the water; the cries of the remaining crew and the firing of her guns every half minute for assistance filled him with dread and terror.

To this day some say that the strange sounds borne on the wind around Deal are the moans of the waking dead devoured by the Goodwins.

Deal, Kent.

Not just vanity

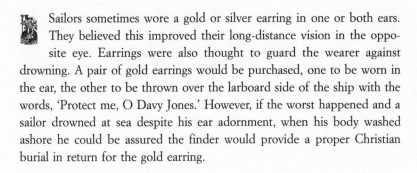

Sailors sometimes wore a gold or silver earring in one or both ears. They believed this improved their long-distance vision in the opposite eye. Earrings were also thought to guard the wearer against drowning. A pair of gold earrings would be purchased, one to be worn in the ear, the other to be thrown over the larboard side of the ship with the words, 'Protect me, O Davy Jones.' However, if the worst happened and a sailor drowned at sea despite his ear adornment, when his body washed ashore he could be assured the finder would provide a proper Christian burial in return for the gold earring.

A voice from the sea

At the turn of the nineteenth century a Cornish lass called Sarah Polgrain had an affair with a sailor known as Yorkshire Jack. When Sarah's husband died he was initially thought to be a victim of cholera, but it was later found that she had poisoned him with arsenic. Sarah was condemned to death by hanging.

She was granted her last wish that Yorkshire Jack be allowed to accompany her to the scaffold. Just as the rope was about to be placed around her neck, Jack kissed her and the two embraced for the last time. Spectators nearby heard Sarah say, 'You will?' and Jack agree.

After Sarah's execution Jack went back to sea, but the once jovial seaman became ill-tempered and agitated. His shipmates often saw him nervously looking over his shoulder.

One morning, as Jack's ship neared home, he confided to one of them, 'When I was on the scaffold that morning talking to Sarah Polgrain, she made me promise on my oath that on this very day, at midnight, I would marry her. Thinking to humour her, and supposing trouble to have unhinged her mind, I agreed. But I know now that she was quite sane and much in earnest. Not being able to wed me in the flesh she means to bind me to her for ever in the spirit.'

That night, eerie footsteps were heard in the vicinity of Jack's hammock. Jack arose as if in a trance and went on deck. He calmly walked to the bulwarks, then leapt into the sea. The shocked watch on deck saw two white faces in the dark waters for a brief moment, and then they were gone.

> TOE THE LINE – keep within the limits of defined behaviour. DERIVATION: the space between deck planks was sealed with a mixture of pitch and oakum. These formed a series of parallel lines 15 cm apart, running the length of the deck. When the crew were ordered to fall in for inspection they mustered in a given area of the deck and stood with their toes just touching a particular seam.

THE PATAGONIAN GIANTS

The region of Patagonia in South America first came to European notice through an account of Ferdinand Magellan's 1520 expedition.

He probably took the name from Patagon, an uncivilised character in a Spanish tale of chivalry he was known to enjoy reading.

Antonio Pigafetta was a wealthy Venetian scholar who accompanied Magellan on his expeditions as a supernumerary and kept a detailed account of his adventures. Pigafetta reported meeting with the inhabitants of Patagonia, who he claimed were over 3.5m in height. This supposed race of giants coloured European perceptions of the strange and remote area for well over two centuries. On early charts of the New World the name Patagonia is sometimes accompanied by the legend *regio gigantum*, region of the giants.

Antonio Pigafetta.

This belief in a race of Goliaths was reinforced by other reports. One of these appeared in the book *Voyages Round the World in His Majesty's Ship the Dolphin*, an allegedly official account of Commodore John Byron's voyage of circumnavigation aboard HMS *Dolphin*, which became an overnight bestseller.

In 1773 on behalf of the Admiralty John Hawkesworth published a sober and analytical three-volume account of English explorers' journals of Patagonia, including those of James Cook and Byron. This work showed conclusively that the people Byron and Cook had encountered were tall, around 2m, but by no means giants.

DARKLING FORERUNNER OF STORMS

 Young Teazer is a ghost ship which locals say blazes, explodes and vanishes around the coast of Nova Scotia in Canada. Usually seen at sunset or moonset, it is a darkling forerunner of storms.

The original *Teazer* was an American privateer commanded by Frederick Johnson that sailed out of New York under a letter of marque (a licence for a privately owned ship to cruise and make prizes of enemy vessels) in the War of 1812. She was captured and burnt by the Royal Navy. The seamen were imprisoned and her officers were paroled awaiting prisoner exchange. As part of the parole the officers gave their solemn word they would not take part in privateering again.

Johnson violated this and sailed in *Teazer*'s successor, *Young Teazer*. This second ship, which sported a figurehead of a carved alligator with jaws agape, was a more powerful privateer; on her maiden voyage from Portland, Maine, she caused considerable destruction to trade and commerce.

On 27 June 1813 she was chased by three British naval ships and finally trapped in Mahone Bay, west of Halifax. The wind died, and boarding parties in five naval cutters were launched to take her, but before they could do so she exploded and flew apart in a sheet of flame. Preferring death to capture, Johnson had put a firebrand to the powder magazine. Of the crew of 38 only eight survived.

Each year during Mahone Bay's Classic Boat Festival there is a re-enactment of the chase and the burning of *Young Teazer*.

> **FIRST-RATE** – of the highest quality. DERIVATION: in a scheme dating from the mid-eighteenth century, the mighty warships of the Royal Navy were rated (classified) on a scale from one to six, based on the ordnance they carried. First-rates were the largest of the ships, carrying 100 or more guns.

EYES TO FIND THE WAY

 One of the abiding images of the grand sailing ship is her majestic curtseying to Neptune as she enters his domain, outward bound, her figurehead standing out proudly. The origins of the familiar carved and painted ornamentation on her bow are to be found in the very early days of seafaring and are probably twofold: homage to the gods to ensure a fair passage and the treatment of the ship as a living thing who needed eyes to find her way across the water.

Figureheads have always been held in great affection by sailors and a ship without a figurehead was considered unlucky. It was believed that a ship with a figurehead could not sink.

In the Royal Navy the lion was almost the standard figurehead for the first three decades of the 1700s. By the middle of the century, the human figure had displaced the lion as the most popular emblem, at least for smaller vessels. Lord Sandwich, First Lord of the Admiralty from 1771 to 1782, introduced many classical names for ships in the Royal Navy and their figure-heads reflected this.

In 1796 figureheads were prohibited on new ships and had to be replaced with an abstract scroll or billet head. This order was not strictly observed, however. In fact, figureheads were still being fitted right up into the twen-tieth century. On 8 December 1900 the last Royal Navy ship with a figure-head, HMS *Espiegle*, was launched at Sheerness. She proudly bore a carved female figure in garments of blue, green and gold.

One famous figurehead is that of HMS *Victory*. The design features two cupids supporting the royal coat of arms surmounted with the royal crown. The arms bear the inscription of the Order of the Garter, 'Shame to him who evil thinks.' During the Battle of Trafalgar the starboard figure had its leg shot away, and the port figure, its arm.

The merchant navy followed naval practice fairly closely up until about 1800. The advent of the clipper ship saw a trend for female forms, often with one or both breasts bared. Sailors thought women on board were gener-ally unlucky, but a half-naked woman was believed to be able to charm a storm at sea.

A figurehead, as the personification of the ship's spirit, should never be desecrated. When the wooden hat of the Duke of Brunswick, figurehead of HMS *Brunswick*, was shot away during the Glorious First of June, Captain Harvey at once handed the ship's carpenter his own cocked hat to be hammered into place on the duke's bald pate.

The famous clipper *Cutty Sark*, now in permanent dry dock in Green-wich, has a bare-breasted Nannie, the witch of Robert Burns's poem, reaching out, in her pursuit of Tam o' Shanter, for the tail of his mare Meg. In the ship's glory days, after one particular sea passage in which she had indeed gone like a witch, a tail of teased rope yarns was fastened into Nannie's hand, an addition that remains to this day. Other famous figureheads include *Golden Hinde*'s gilded deer, *Mary Rose*'s unicorn, *Revenge*'s lion and the image of King Edgar for *Sovereign of the Sea*. Many figureheads have survived and been preserved in maritime museums around the world.

NELSON'S BLOOD

The myth persists that after he died on board HMS *Victory* of his wounds sustained at the Battle of Trafalgar, Nelson's body was preserved in a cask of rum before being returned to England for burial. On the way home, according to some versions of the story, the sailors on board *Victory* drilled a small hole in the cask and drank the rum, hoping to imbibe some of his strength and courage. To this day in the Royal Navy rum is known as 'Nelson's blood'.

Most sailors were committed to the deep if they died at sea, but Nelson had made it plain that he did not wish such a fate. This presented surgeon Beatty with the task of preserving the body. There was not sufficient lead on board to make an airtight coffin, and he had neither the equipment nor the knowledge for embalming. After cutting off Nelson's hair for Lady Hamilton, Beatty placed the shirt-clad body in a water leaguer, the largest barrel aboard. He filled this with brandy, probably taken from a French prize, and lashed the barrel to the mainmast on the middle deck. There, it was guarded day and night by an armed marine.

En route to Gibraltar the sentry got the fright of his life when the lid of the barrel began to rise up, no doubt as a result of the body's release of internal gases. At Gibraltar it was found that Nelson's body had absorbed a quantity of the brandy, which was replaced with spirits of wine, a better preservative. Owing to bad weather the long voyage back to England took over four weeks and during the course of it the cask was renewed twice with two parts of brandy to one part spirits of wine.

In England Nelson's body was placed in the '*L'Orient* coffin' (see page 48), which in turn was sealed into an ornate outer coffin covered in black velvet and gold chasings, and the nation's hero lay in state within the Painted Hall at Greenwich Hospital before the state funeral. Admiral Nelson was finally laid to rest in St Paul's Cathedral.

The Battle of Trafalgar.

TURNING A BLIND EYE – knowing what is happening but ignoring it. DERIVATION: at the Battle of Copenhagen Admiral Parker hoisted a signal to Nelson to discontinue the action. Nelson, in one of the most famous acts of insubordination in the annals of the Royal Navy, turned to one of his officers and said, 'I have only one eye. I have a right to be blind sometimes.' He then put the glass to his blind eye and said, 'I really do not see the signal.' He went on to win the battle.

ESTEEMED BY LAWYERS AND OLD SALTS ALIKE

 The caul, the thin membrane covering the heads of some new-born children, has long been held by mariners to bring good luck. It was also believed to guard against drowning and shipwreck.

As long as the person born with the caul kept it with him, the life-saving powers would protect him. If it was sold, they would pass to the buyer.

In February 1813 an advertisement in *The Times* offered a caul for 12 guineas. It was not unusual to see them for sale this way. Another paper announced the sale of a caul 'having been afloat with its late owner forty years, through the periods of a seaman's life and he died at last in his bed, at his place of birth'.

Having paid handsomely for them, sailors would often sew them into their canvas trousers. One old tar with a caul secreted on his person in this way was told his amulet was a 'vulgar error'. He replied: 'A vulgar error saving me from Davy Jones is as good as any other.'

Admiral Smyth in his classic book of nautical terms published in 1867 observes that a caul was sought as eagerly by the Roman lawyers as by modern voyagers. The lawyers apparently believed it would guarantee they would be eloquent and successful in all their cases.

SHE

We always call a ship a 'she' and not without a reason
For she displays a well-shaped knee regardless of the season
She scorns the man whose heart is faint and shows him no pity
And like a girl she needs the paint to keep her looking pretty

Anon.

A ship has long been traditionally called 'she' by most seafarers (the Russians, Germans and French excepted). No one knows how and when this first started, but given the dependence the early seafarers had on their ships for life and sustenance, the use of the feminine form is perhaps not surprising. To this day mariners feel a deep affection for any ship that has safely borne them at her bosom over the ocean, and it seems only natural to them to call a ship 'she'.

Another anonymous explanation goes like this:

A boat is called she because there's always a great deal of bustle around her... because there's usually a gang of men around... because she has a waist and stays... because she takes a lot of paint to keep her looking good... because it's not the initial expense that breaks you, it's the upkeep... because she is all decked out... because it takes a good man to handle her right... because she shows her topsides, hides her bottom, and, when coming into port, always heads for the buoys.

When Lloyd's List, founded in 1734, announced in 2002 that it would change the gender of ships from 'she' to 'it' the decision generated considerable opposition from traditionalists. The Royal Navy responded that it would continue to use the female pronoun, and in the face of overwhelming protest Lloyds List subsequently reversed its decision.

IN SOMEONE'S BLACK BOOK – contravening someone's personal code of conduct. DERIVATION: the Admiralty Black Book, dating from the fourteenth century, is an ancient volume concerned with naval laws and discipline. It is preserved in the Public Records Office at Kew, London.

THE MERFOLK

 Seafarers crossing the vast expanse of oceans spoke of a world below the waves populated by merfolk. These creatures were half human, half fish. If they were tormented they could wreak terrible revenge.

Mermaids would sing to sailors, distracting them from their work and causing shipwrecks, or sometimes inadvertently squeeze the life out of drowning men while trying to rescue them.

There are a number of recorded historical sightings of mermaids. Columbus reported seeing three mermaids on his first voyage to the Americas. On 4 January 1493 he wrote in his log that the female forms 'rose high out of the sea, but were not as beautiful as they are represented'.

In 1608 the English navigator Henry Hudson was sailing off the Arctic coast of Russia and made this log entry on 15 June:

This morning, one of our companie looking over board saw a mermaid, and calling up some of the companie to see her, one more came up, and by that time shee was close to the ship's side, looking earnestly upon the men: a little after a Sea came and overturned her. From the navill upward, her backe and breasts were like a woman's... her boday as big as any one of us; her skin very white; and long haire hanging down behinde, of colour blacke; in her going down they saw her tayle, which was like the tayle of a Porposse, and speckled like a Macrell.

Six years later in the Caribbean another captain, John Smith, spotted a mermaid 'swimming about with all possible grace'.

Nineteenth-century advertisement.

Dutch sailors caught a 'sea wyf' off the coast of Borneo and kept her in a large vat for nearly a week. She was known as the Mermaid of Amboine.

Throughout the nineteenth century a number of so-called mermaids were exhibited. One, brought to London by Captain Eades of Boston in 1822, was visited by Sir Everard Home, president of the Royal College of Surgeons, who pronounced it a 'palpable imposition' – the cranium of an orang-utang, teeth, jaws and trunk of a baboon, padded breasts and lower body of a large fish. Nevertheless, nearly 400 people paid a shilling each to view it at the Turf Coffee House, St James. In July 1842 a Dr J. Griffin arrived in New York with a specimen that was to become known as 'the Feejee Mermaid'. The mummified body was exhibited by the showman P.T. Barnum for the next 20 years.

*I*F HE'S WHISTLING, IT'S DUFF FOR DINNER

 Many mariners' beliefs concerned the weather. Sometimes a horse-shoe was nailed upside down to the mast of a ship to avert storms and shipwreck. Nelson was said to have had one on the mainmast of HMS *Victory*.

Seamen were particularly anxious about squalls. It would certainly bring bad luck not to follow the advice of the old ditty:

> When the rain's before the wind
> Strike your tops'ls, reef your main
> When the wind's before the rain
> Shake 'em out and go again

Among American sailors felines were thought creatures of ill omen: should cats frolic aboard this was a sure sign of a storm; if they washed behind their ears this would bring rain, and if one was seen climbing the rigging the ship was doomed!

The appearance of a waterspout, often accompanied by flashes of lightning and a sulphurous smell, generated terror aboard ship. Sailors knew the wind which blew in sudden gusts in their vicinity was sufficient to capsize small vessels carrying a large spread of sail. One remedy against such disaster that was popular with the mariners who accompanied Columbus was to hold a knife with a black handle in one hand and, reading the Gospel of St John, cut the air with the knife afore the waterspout.

A Strange Light at the Masthead

The phenomenon of St Elmo's fire, which goes by many names, has long been seen as an omen at sea. St Elmo was the patron saint of Mediterranean sailors. He died at sea during a storm, and in his last moments he promised the crew he would return and show himself to them in some form if they were destined to survive the storm. Soon after he died a strange light appeared at the masthead.

Sailors read various interpretations into the configuration of St Elmo's fire. One light is a warning of a storm, two lights are a sign that the storm centre has passed, but three lights portend a gale of overwhelming proportions. If the lights go up the mast, good weather is expected, but if they go down things will get worse. It is dangerous to attempt to touch the light, or even go near to it, and if it shines like a halo around a man's head his speedy death is certain! Columbus gave cheer to his disgruntled crew on the voyage to America by pointing to St Elmo's fire at the masthead and predicting an early end to their perils.

St Elmo's fire strikes a ship.

Generally, whistling was discouraged in ships. When becalmed, scratching a backstay and whistling softly might entice a useful breeze, but it was to be avoided if the weather was threatening to get dirty; it could annoy Saint Anthony, the patron saint of wind, and a strong blow could come on.

In the Royal Navy whistling was banned at sea, as it could be confused with orders given by the bosun's whistle. There was one exception to this, however. When making the boiled pudding known as duff, the ship's cook was traditionally made to whistle so that he could not surreptitiously eat the raisins destined for the popular treat.

WITCHCRAFT OVER THE WATER

Witches, taking the shape of waves, have ever been the nemesis of sailors. They stop ships, turn the wind and raise general havoc, often using cats as familiars. Witchcraft was sometimes attributed to people who had good reason to feel malevolence against the ship, such as landladies whose bill had not been paid by some of the men on board.

When Anne of Denmark was crossing the North Sea in 1589, en route to marry James I of England, a coven of witches at Leith in Scotland raised a storm that interrupted the voyage. A witch hunt was instigated, and under torture a number of Danish and Scottish women confessed to sorcery. One claimed that she had taken a cat and christened it and then bound several parts of a dead man to it. In the night she and her fellow witches threw the unfortunate animal into the sea.

It was popularly believed in Scotland that the Spanish Armada met defeat on account of the witches on the island of Mull who brought the storms that scuttled many of Philip's ships.

On trial in 1684, Edward Man of the merchant vessel *Neptune* attempted to explain his incompetence in bringing her to Milford Haven instead of London by telling the court that he had been bewitched by the ship's cat and that it was 'the Divell had brought them thither'.

Sometimes witches sold mariners special powers in the form of knotted cords so they could personally influence the weather. As the knots were loosened the wind increased, until at the untying of the last knot a gale arose.

Witches raise a storm at sea, sixteenth-century engraving.

> CHOCK-A-BLOCK – completely full. DERIVATION: when a block and tackle has reached the point where the two blocks come together it cannot go any further.

*S*ALUTING THE QUARTERDECK

Custom dictates that in any naval ship the quarterdeck (the upper deck from the main mast to right aft) symbolises the Service and is the focus for its ceremonial. In the Middle Ages a crucifix was placed in this area, and was the first object seen when boarding a ship. Officers and men would remove their headgear at the figure of Christ, and this probably explains the practice, which survives today, of saluting the quarterdeck. A salute is also given on entering a ship, for in the days of sail coming aboard over the bulwarks would place you on the quarterdeck. The Royal Naval College at Dartmouth has a large hall, somewhat church-like in appearance, known as the Quarterdeck, which lies at the heart of the college.

*D*ENIZENS OF THE DEEP

> Below the thunders of the upper deep
> Far far beneath in the abysmal sea
> His ancient, dreamless, uninvaded sleep
> The Kraken sleepeth...

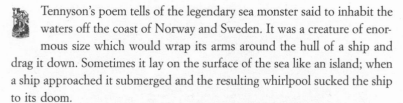

Tennyson's poem tells of the legendary sea monster said to inhabit the waters off the coast of Norway and Sweden. It was a creature of enormous size which would wrap its arms around the hull of a ship and drag it down. Sometimes it lay on the surface of the sea like an island; when a ship approached it submerged and the resulting whirlpool sucked the ship to its doom.

Other sea monsters sighted have included sea dragons and sea serpents, which could be slimy or scaly and often spouted jets of water.

Sir Henry Gilbert claimed to have encountered a lion-like monster with glaring eyes on his return voyage to England from Newfoundland in 1583.

A Very Terrible Sea Animal

Hans Egede, a missionary on a voyage to the western coast of Greenland in July 1734, reported: '[There] appeared a very terrible sea-animal, which raised itself so high above the water that its head reached above our maintop. It had a long, sharp snout, and blew like a whale... on the lower part it was formed like a snake... it raised its tail above the water, a whole ship length from its body.'

Perhaps the most famous sighting occurred on 6 August 1848, when HMS *Daedalus* was on passage to England from the East Indies. Midshipman Satoris reported seeing something very unusual in the sea to officer-of-the-watch Lieutenant Edgar Drummond. The two came to the conclusion that they had seen a sea serpent and informed the captain.

The ship reached Plymouth on 4 October. Someone on board leaked the story to the press and *The Times* printed a lively account of the sighting. Until this time the captain of *Daedalus* Peter M'Quhae had kept silent, nervous no doubt of the reaction of the navy to such a tale, and for this reason the incident had not been logged officially. However, he was ordered to report to Admiral Sir W.H. Gage, who demanded an explanation of what he had read in the newspaper. M'Quhae produced Drummond's journal and

Daedulus and the sea serpent.

a picture of an enormous serpent with head and shoulders about a metre above the surface of the sea. The creature was described 'as nearly as we could approximate by comparing it with the length of what our main topsail yard would show in the water, there was at least 60 feet of the animal *à fleur d'eau*, no portion of which was, to our perception, used in propelling it through the water... It passed so close under our lee quarter that had it been a man of my acquaintance, I would have easily recognised his features with the naked eye...'

The sighting caused a stir in the scientific community. Sir Richard Owen, curator of the Hunterian Museum, argued that it was a seal. Others suggested an upside-down canoe or a giant squid.

Could those aboard *Daedalus* have met a living creature of some unknown species?

THE BUZZARD'S CODE

Olivier Levasseur was a French pirate nicknamed La Buse, meaning the buzzard, for the alacrity with which he threw himself at his enemies.

His greatest prize was the capture, in 1721 off the island of La Réunion, of *Nossa Senhora do Cabo*, a Portuguese vessel loaded with gold and jewels belonging to the retiring viceroy of Goa. The booty included a magnificent solid gold cross, 2 m high and encrusted with diamonds, emeralds and rubies, known as 'The Fiery Cross of Goa'.

The 17-line cipher.

It is believed that La Buse concealed the treasure somewhere along the northeastern coast of Mahe, the principal island of the Seychelles archipelago.

Nine years after this incredible haul Levasseur was captured and hanged. But he did not depart from life without some drama. Legend has it that at the gallows he threw out some parchment maps and documents identifying the location of where he had buried the treasure. They were in code, however, and he called to the crowd, 'Find my treasure, he who may understand it.'

Several copies were made of these papers, which included a cipher containing 17 lines of Greek and Hebrew letters.

The hunt was taken up in the 1950s by Reginald Cruise-Wilkins, a former Coldstream Guardsman, who eventually believed he had broken much of the code and that the hoard lies somewhere in the vicinity of Bel Ombre on Mahe. Before his death in 1977 he passed the treasure hunter's baton to his son, John, who continues the search for what is perhaps the greatest treasure ever to fall into the hands of a pirate. Its value today could exceed several hundred million pounds.

> IN THE OFFING – about to happen. DERIVATION: a ship would be trapped against the land if an enemy came out of the offing. This was the sea area beyond anchoring ground but visible from the coast.

*F*AMOUS LAST WORDS

Nelson's last words were neither 'Kiss me, Hardy' nor 'Kismet, Hardy'. Both versions have a wide currency, but in fact Hardy was not even present at the moment of the admiral's death as he had been called back on deck.

When Nelson was wounded and carried below, Hardy remained on the quarterdeck directing the battle. It was well over an hour before he could clamber down to see his friend. Hardy was able to tell Nelson that they had taken 12 or 14 of the enemy vessels, and then he returned to his post.

Another hour passed before Hardy could find time to visit Nelson for a second time. They shook hands and Nelson told Hardy to be sure to anchor. After reminding him to take care of 'poor Lady Hamilton' he said, 'Kiss me, Hardy.' Hardy responded with a kiss on the cheek and then, after a brief reflective pause, a second on the forehead. Nelson's last words to his captain were 'God bless you, Hardy'. Hardy then withdrew and returned to the quarterdeck.

Nelson's life was by now draining fast and he was drifting in and out of consciousness. With his eyes closed he murmured softly, 'Thank God I have done my duty.' These were his last words.

Chapter 5.

Maritime
MISFORTUNES

Maritime
MISFORTUNES

Introduction

When Port Royal, Jamaica, 'the richest and wickedest city in the world', was swept into the sea in 1692, many saw it as retribution for an immoral existence. But the sea is not an agent of revenge, nor is it cruel; it is indifferent, an elemental, primal force. The seaman turned novelist Joseph Conrad once said, 'If you want to know the age of the earth, look upon the sea in a storm.' And the poet Lord Byron described the sea as 'dark-heaving, boundless, endless, and sublime. The image of Eternity...'

Since the early days of sail countless brave souls who have set forth on the bounding main have not returned. It might be supposed that sea battles have taken the largest toll in human life, but this is not the case. During 20 years of war between 1793 and 1813 approximately 100,000 men in the Royal Navy died – 6.3 per cent from enemy action, 12.2 per cent from shipwreck and other disasters and 81.5 per cent from disease or accident.

Fire at sea was particularly feared by sailors. In ships made almost entirely of combustibles – wood, canvas and tarred cordage just waiting for a flame – a small blaze could very quickly become an inferno. One of the unforgettable images of the Battle of the Nile is the fire aboard *L'Orient*, the massive French flagship. Such was the amazement on both sides at the intensity of the conflagration and the resulting explosion that the entire battle actually stopped for a short time. But of all the causes of death at sea one looms above all the rest – scurvy. The dreaded affliction was responsible for more deaths at sea than all the other causes combined, and it probably killed two million sailors during the Golden Age of Sail.

'The Shipwreck', a nineteenth-century engraving.

'*A*N ERROR OF HIS PROFESSION'

It should have been a glorious homecoming after successful operations against the French at Toulon, but it became one of the worst disasters in the history of the Royal Navy. In October 1707 the Mediterranean Fleet under Admiral Sir Cloudesley Shovell in HMS *Association* set sail from Gibraltar bound for England.

As they neared the English Channel bad weather made them unsure of their position. The admiral consulted his navigators, who believed they were west of Ushant (Ile d'Ouessant) off the Brittany peninsula, well south of any hazards – but in reality they were 160 km north. Shortly afterwards *Association*, *Romney* and *Eagle* were driven on to rocks off the Scilly Isles and sank with the loss of all on board except the quartermaster of *Romney*. Over 1,300 perished, all down to a combination of bad weather and the inability of mariners in those times to determine their position with accuracy.

Many tales have endured over the centuries about this tragic event, ranging from Shovell hanging a seaman who tried to warn him of impending danger to a local woman murdering the admiral when he was washed ashore in order to steal a large emerald ring that he wore on his hand.

Shovell was initially buried in a simple grave at Porth Hellick, a small community on one of the Scilly isles, but his body was later exhumed and reburied in Westminster Abbey. One newspaper of the day commented, 'It was very unhappy for an admiral, reputed one of the greatest sea commanders we ever had, to die by an error of his profession.'

Some good did come out of this tragedy – the Admiralty instigated a search for a way of calculating longitude. In 1714 they offered a prize of £20,000 for a solution, but it was many decades before a way was found of determining an accurate position with a chronometer (see page 81).

THE PIRATE CITY THAT WAS SWALLOWED BY THE SEA

Port Royal on the southern coast of Jamaica was claimed by England in 1655 and soon earned the title 'the richest and wickedest city in the world'.

Its location in the middle of the Caribbean made it an ideal base for trade, and buccaneers too were attracted to its large harbour, which was perfect for launching raids on Spanish settlements. Among its most notorious pirates was Henry Morgan, who in a seventeenth-century version of poacher turned gamekeeper was appointed lieutenant-governor of Jamaica in 1674.

By the 1660s most of the 6,500 residents of Port Royal were buccaneers, cut-throats and prostitutes. There was one drinking house for every ten residents, along with all manner of merchants, goldsmiths, artists – and even several places of worship.

Den of Iniquity

Outrageous behaviour was rife in Port Royal. Men paid 500 pieces of eight just to see a common strumpet naked. Some bought a pipe of wine, placed it in the street and then obliged passers-by to drink. Prostitutes with names like No-Conscience Nan, Salt-Beef Peg and Buttock-de-Clink Jenny could hold their own in the rough male company – and amassed fortunes. The most famous was Mary Carleton. A contemporary wrote of her: 'A stout frigate she was or else she never could have endured so many batteries and assaults... she was as common as a barber's chair; no sooner was one out, but another was in.'

In its heyday there were around 1,000 residences in Port Royal, many of them large houses with multi-storey brick structures. It was said that the splendour of the finest homes was comparable to those in London.

On the morning of 7 June 1692 Port Royal fell victim to a series of natural disasters, beginning with a massive earthquake. The town was built on the sandy Palisades spit, which was intrinsically unstable, and the western side of the settlement was swallowed by sea, along with all the buildings and inhabitants. Then came an enormous tidal wave which swept away more of the town. When the water subsided only 10 hectares of Port Royal remained. Around 2,000 lost their lives instantly, and a further 3,000 succumbed to injury and disease over the next few weeks.

One astonishing tale of survival concerns Lewis Galdy, a French Huguenot who had settled in Jamaica. The inscription on his tombstone relates: 'He was swallowed up in the great earthquake... and by the providence of God was by another shock thrown into the sea and miraculously saved by swimming until a boat took him up.'

Port Royal, Jamaica.

'LIQUID FIRE'

A lightning strike aboard a sailing ship could have horrific consequences – fire, explosion, even the incineration of hapless sailors. Some, who weren't killed outright, suffered paralysis, terrible burns or blindness.

On 21 November 1790 the naval town of Portsmouth in southern England experienced an extraordinary storm. Lightning rolled along the ground 'like a body of liquid fire'. The 74-gun ship of the line HMS *Elephant* was moored in the harbour and narrowly avoided complete destruction when she was struck by the lightning. The maintopmast exploded, but it did not plunge through the quarterdeck, as it was still held by the top ropes.

Lightning could strike anywhere around the world. Because of his command of languages, the Revd. Alexander Scott, who was later to serve as Nelson's private secretary aboard HMS *Victory,* sometimes undertook duties outside the normal remit of a naval chaplain. In 1802 he was aboard a former French prize *Topaze* in the West Indies, having been sent to St Domingo (now Haiti) to gather intelligence from French officers. While returning from this assignment he was involved in a freak accident.

One evening just after midnight the vessel was struck by lightning during a severe thunderstorm. It split the mizzenmast, killing and wounding 14 men, then descended into the cabin in which Scott was sleeping. He suffered an electric shock and the hooks suspending his hammock melted, flinging him to the ground. Simultaneously the lightning caused an explosion in a cache of small-arms powder stored above him. The resultant blast knocked out several of Scott's teeth, injured his jaw and affected his hearing and eyesight. For a time he was paralysed on one side of his body. Scott did recover from these injuries, but for the rest of his life he suffered from 'nerves'.

A study in 1851 of ships in the Royal Navy catalogued the extensive damage caused to the fleet by lightning. One six-year period, from 1809 to 1815, saw 30 ships of the line and 15 frigates disabled. And the merchant marine also suffered; there were vivid reports in the press of the loss of shipping and valuable cargo.

Lightning conductors were not entirely trusted at first; they were believed by some to draw down upon a ship more 'electric fluid' than they could transmit safely to earth. Trials in 1831 demonstrated the utility of these devices, but they did not always prevent disasters. Tragedies continued to occur, especially when the ship was at an angle and other spiky protuberances such as the bowsprit and the driver boom end could attract lightning.

POOPED – visibly overwhelmed by exhaustion.
DERIVATION: the poop is the high deck aft above the quarterdeck, found in the larger sailing ships. A ship is pooped when a heavy sea breaks over her stern while she is running before the wind in a gale – a very dangerous situation because the vessel's speed in this circumstance is approximately the same as the following sea. She therefore loses steerage way and becomes uncontrollable as the wave rampages down her deck.

$\mathcal{A}$DMIRAL HOSIER'S GHOST

In March 1726 Vice-Admiral Francis Hosier was appointed to command a squadron bound for the West Indies. His orders were to prevent the Spanish treasure ships sailing home from Porto Bello. However, when Hosier's ships arrived, the Spaniards simply sent their treasure back to Panama, leaving the galleons empty. In the absence of further orders Hosier blockaded these ships from June to December, losing great numbers of his men to the dreaded yellow fever, the 'black vomit'.

With so many casualties to disease he was forced to return to his base in Jamaica, where the ships were cleared out and new men were recruited to replace the dead. However, the contagion remained and over the next six months, while the squadron was blockading other Spanish ports, the casualties continued to mount. Out of 4,750 men over 4,000 died.

Eventually Hosier succumbed to the disease himself, and after lingering for ten long days he died on 27 August 1727 in Jamaica, as did his immediate successors, Commodore St Lo and Rear Admiral Hopson. Hosier's body was embalmed and brought back in the ballast of a sloop inaptly named *Happy*. He was buried in his native Deptford.

Hosier achieved posthumous fame in 1740 when Richard Glover published a poem, 'Admiral Hosier's Ghost', a blatantly political piece. Glover used Hosier's fate to support attacks on the Walpole government. In the poem (which later became a popular song) Hosier's ghost appears to Edward Vernon, after his successful capture of Porto Bello, which had eluded Hosier.

Heed, oh heed our fatal story
I am Hosier's injured ghost
You who now have purchased
 glory
At this place where I was lost.

Contemporary satirical print.

$\mathcal{A}$ TERRIBLE SCENE OF DEVASTATION

 The frigate HMS *Amphion* had just completed repairs in Plymouth dockyard, Devon, and as she was due to sail the next day, she had more than 100 visitors and relatives on board in addition to her crew, making a total of about 400 persons.

Captain Israel Pellew was dining in his cabin with his first lieutenant and Captain Swaffield of a Dutch man-o'-war. At about 4 p.m. in the afternoon on 22 September 1796 a violent shock was felt in the town and the sky lit up bright red as a massive explosion blew the ship apart. People ran to the dockyard and witnessed a terrible scene of devastation. Strewn in all directions were splintered timbers, broken rigging and blackened, mangled bodies.

At the instant of the explosion Pellew and his guests were thrown violently off their chairs. Pellew rushed to the window and climbed out. He managed to escape virtually unharmed and was picked up by a boat. The first lieutenant, too, got clear with only minor injuries. Captain Swaffield, however, perished. His body was found a month later with his skull fractured.

There were some miraculous escapes among the crew. At the moment of the explosion the marine at the captain's cabin door was looking at his watch – it was dashed from his hands and he was stunned senseless. He knew nothing more until he found himself safe on shore, having suffered only slightly. The boatswain was standing on the cathead directing his men at work when he felt himself suddenly carried off his feet into the air. He fell into the water and lost consciousness. When he came to, he found he was entangled in some rigging and had suffered a broken arm, but he managed to extricate himself and was picked up by a boat.

Apart from Pellew, the only survivors were two lieutenants, a boatswain, three or four seamen, a marine, a woman and a child. The child was discovered clutched to her mother's lifeless bosom; the lower half of her body had been blown to pieces.

The cause of this disaster was never established, but many believe the ship's gunner was stealing gunpowder, which accidentally ignited.

$\mathcal{M}$AN OVERBOARD AND THEN SOME ...

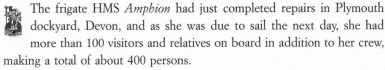 A fall from the rigging was usually fatal if the seaman hit the decks. Landing in the water he had a chance of survival if he could be found quickly enough.

On occasion the attempt to rescue a man from the water led to greater disaster. On 24 November 1804 a signal was made for the fleet moored at Torbay, a naval anchorage in southern England, to get under way. It was a very dark night, and while raising the anchor of HMS *Venerable* a master's mate and a seaman fell overboard. A boat was instantly lowered to try to save them, but in the confusion it filled with water and the rescue crew were thrown in the sea.

At that moment another ship loomed up in the dark and evasive action was taken to avoid collision. Then *Venerable* began drifting, stern first, into the shore and grounded on rocks and hard sand. Water poured into the doomed vessel.

The cutter *Frisk* attempted to take men off *Venerable*, as did other ships' boats, but the weather worsened and the hulk became submerged to the upper gun deck. Then *Frisk* did manage to rescue a number of the men, and a makeshift raft enabled others to get ashore. Some of the sailors still aboard, meanwhile, believing their fate was sealed, broke into the spirit room to seek oblivion in drink.

A court martial was convened on 11 December following the loss of the ship. Captain Hunter, his officers and the ship's company were all honourably acquitted, except for one sailor who was found guilty of drunkenness, disobedience of orders and plundering the officers' baggage. He was sentenced to 200 lashes around the fleet.

HMS Venerable *meets her end at Torbay.*

CUTS A FINE FEATHER – said of a person who is a nifty dresser. DERIVATION: when a ship was sailing well her bow wave looked like a white feather.

'$\mathcal{P}$LAGUE OF THE SEA'

 Scurvy was once the most malignant of all sea diseases. Painful and loathsome in its symptoms, it killed two million sailors during the Golden Age of Sail.

The disease was first observed by the ancient Greek physician Hippocrates. Physical symptoms included black-coloured skin, ulcers, difficulty in breathing, loss of teeth and rotting gums. Sometimes old wounds reopened from injuries sustained decades earlier. Scurvy resulted in strange sensory and psychological effects. When a man was in the last stages of the disease the sound of a gunshot was enough to kill him, while the smell of blossom from the shore could cause him to cry out in agony. The sufferer broke down into tears at the slightest provocation and suffered acute yearnings for the shore.

History records the devastation caused on long sea voyages. Vasco da Gama saw two-thirds of his crew succumb to the disease en route to India in 1499. In 1520 Magellan lost more than 80 per cent of his men to scurvy while crossing the Pacific. The Elizabethan sea explorer Sir Richard Hawkins cursed the disease as 'the plague of the sea and the spoyle of mariners'. In 1740 Commodore Anson led a squadron of five warships on a four-year voyage which turned into the worst sea-borne medical disaster in history. Over half of the 2,000 men who left England with him died from scurvy, and only one vessel of his fleet returned, his flagship HMS *Centurion*.

Many anti-scorbutics that were heralded as cures were in fact useless. Among these were elixir of vitriol – made from sulphuric acid, spirit of wine, sugar, cinnamon, ginger and other spices, and Ward pills, a violent diuretic. Some believed that going ashore and being half buried in earth would result in a cure. Spruce beer, made from the leaves of the conifer, was officially issued in the North American station.

James Cook succeeded in circumnavigating the world in 1768–71 in *Endeavour* without losing a single man to scurvy. He was a great believer in regular doses of wort of malt, but this would not have been effective as a remedy. He did ensure that his crew's diet was supplemented with fresh fruit and vegetables, but probably the one truly anti-scorbutic measure he took was to prohibit the eating of the fat skimmed off the vats used to boil salt meat. Cook took this measure as he believed the practice was unhealthy but we now know that fat interacts with copper to produce a substance that prevents the gut from absorbing vitamins.

The Scottish naval surgeon James Lind proved the disease could be treated with citrus fruits in experiments he described in his 1753 book *A Treatise of the Scurvy*. Scurvy was not eradicated from the Royal Navy, however, until the chairman of the navy's Sick and Hurt Board, Gilbert Blane, finally put the prescription of fresh lemons to use during the Napoleonic Wars. Other navies soon adopted this successful solution.

Earlier experiments with the use of limes, which were not nearly as effective as lemons in preventing scurvy, gave rise to the nickname 'limey' for British sailors.

James Lind.

THE EVENT THAT INSPIRED *MOBY DICK*

By the beginning of the nineteenth century whaling had made Nantucket, Massachusetts, one of the richest localities in the United States. In 1819 the whaling ship *Essex* under 29-year-old Captain George Pollard left for the whaling grounds of the South Pacific with a crew of 20 men. The voyage was expected to take two and a half years.

On 20 November 1820 spouts were sighted, and as usual the ship gave chase and launched the dories, leaving just a skeleton crew aboard. Suddenly a huge bull whale breached, spouted and swam at high speed towards the ship, ramming it at the waterline near the bow and throwing all those on board to the deck. The creature then surfaced beside the ship, shook itself and dived again. Then it came back for a second attack and the ship rolled over on to her beam-ends. Hastily returning to the ship, Pollard asked, 'My God, what is the matter?' and was told, 'We've been stove by a whale!' *Essex* stayed afloat for two days, after which the crew had to abandon ship and take their chances in the whaleboats.

After 22 days they landed on uninhabited Henderson Island, within the modern-day Pitcairn Islands. They soon exhausted the natural resources there, however, and all but three of them decided to press on.

Back at sea, one by one the men died. At first they were thrown overboard, but as time went on and more died, hunger drove the sailors to eat the corpses. In Pollard's boat, however, there had been no natural deaths and the men drew lots to determine who would be sacrificed for the survival of the others. The grim fate befell Pollard's young cousin.

Eventually they were picked up by other whaleboats. After more than 90 days in the tiny craft, in which they drifted some 6,400 km, only eight of the original 21 mariners from the *Essex* had survived.

According to Nantucket legend, years later George Pollard was asked if he had known a man called Owen Coffin. He replied, 'Know 'im? Why bless you, I ate 'im.'

First mate Owen Chase wrote an account of the disaster which inspired Herman Melville to pen his famous novel *Moby Dick*.

Braving the seas to hunt oil-rich sperm whales.

SKYSCRAPER – few cities in the world today are without these majestic buildings soaring skyward. Chicago's Home Insurance Building erected in 1884 was the world's first tall building supported by an internal frame and was dubbed a 'skyscraper' by the press. DERIVATION: the highest sail in a ship, a skyscraper is a small triangular canvas set above the royals in order to maximise the effect of a light wind.

SUNK IN THE SIGHT OF THE KING

 The warship *Mary Rose,* named after Henry VIII's favourite sister and the Tudor emblem, was the pride of the King's fleet, described as 'the flower of all ships that ever sailed'.

Mary Rose had a long and successful career against the French behind her when she sailed from Portsmouth harbour in July 1545 at the head of the English fleet to take on the approaching enemy once again.

King Henry watched from Southsea Castle, just a few hundred metres away. *Mary Rose* fired one broadside at the French and was turning to fire the other broadside when water flooded into her open gunports and she suddenly capsized in full view of the monarch, the screams of the sailors ringing in his ears. Only 30 or so of those on board survived. The official crew of *Mary Rose* was 200 mariners, 185 soldiers and 30 gunners, but one account says there were as many as 700 on board when she sank.

Among those drowned was Vice-Admiral Sir George Carew, whose wife, watching with the king, collapsed in shock. The cry of horror that broke from Henry's lips became seared in the memory of those near him.

There is no agreement as to exactly why the great warship sank. One recent theory puts it down to a French cannonball. Some believe it was indiscipline within the crew. Indeed the last message shouted by George Carew to his uncle Sir Gawen Carew sailing nearby in the *Matthew Gonnson* was, 'I have the sort of knaves I cannot rule.'

Others believe it was due to the gunports being too close to the waterline. It was probably a combination of factors, however, that caused the catastrophe.

The wreck of *Mary Rose* was discovered in 1968, and in 1982, after much underwater preparation, the surviving section of the ship was lifted from the seabed and returned to Portsmouth harbour 437 years after her departure. Now on view in the Historic Dockyard, she is the only sixteenth-century warship on display anywhere in the world.

Mary Rose.

MUTINY!

 During the age of sail the penalty for naval insurrection was hanging at the yardarm. Under the Articles of War, a court martial had first to be convened before such punishment, usually swift and merciless, was administered.

One of the most notorious mutinies to take place in the Royal Navy occurred aboard HMS *Hermione*, a 32-gun frigate. In July 1797 Hugh Pigot became her new captain. He already had a reputation for cruelty, and after a very unjust punishment of one of the crew the others became particularly restless.

On 20 September, patrolling the Mona Passage, a major entry point into the Caribbean, the men prepared to shorten sail for the night. Not content to leave the supervision of this to his officers, Pigot called out through his speaking trumpet that the sailors were slow and that he would flog the last man down on deck. Three younger sailors panicked and slipped in their haste to come down. One broke his fall by landing on the master, injuring him. The others fell senseless at Pigot's feet, and he growled, 'Throw the lubbers overboard.' He then ordered two boatswain's mates to go aloft with knotted ropes to beat the remaining sailors. He had a dozen seamen flogged the next day.

The following night three parties of mutineers took matters into their own hands. One group overpowered the marine on duty outside Pigot's cabin and then forced the door open. Pigot jumped up from his cot in his nightshirt. Grabbing a dirk he put up a strong fight against cutlasses and boarding axes, but soon he was backed into a corner, injured and bleeding.

Meanwhile the alarm had been raised and the third lieutenant, Mr Foreshaw, tried to take control on the quarterdeck, but he was quickly overcome and thrown overboard.

In his cabin, Pigot was subjected to continuous physical and verbal assaults. His cries for mercy were ignored, and he was finally hurled through the stern windows into the sea. His screams of fury and pain could be heard from the shark-infested waters as the ship drew away.

Although some were opposed to taking any more lives, the carnage continued. The maddened ship's company brutally murdered another ten and dispatched them overboard. They then took the ship into La Guaira, Venezuela, a few days' sail away, where they handed it over to the Spanish.

The navy set about seeking retribution, finally bringing 33 to trial and hanging 24 of them. Many eluded capture. *Hermione* was recaptured and returned to naval service. It was decided that she must have a new name, and at first it was to be *Retaliation,* but this was considered too pointed and it was changed to *Retribution.*

Other notorious British naval uprisings were the mutinies at Spithead and the Nore, the latter led by former naval officer turned seaman Richard Parker, and the insurrection against Captain Bligh on board HMS *Bounty,* famously made into five films.

Hanged Without Trial

An incident in the American naval brig USS *Somers,* captained by Alexander Mackenzie, caused a controversy that is still argued over today. Three sailors were hanged in December 1842 aboard the vessel, before a court martial was convened. They were midshipman Philip Spencer, son of the secretary of war, boatswain's mate Samuel Cromwell and seaman Elisha Small. It was alleged that they had planned to take over the ship, throw the officers and loyal crew members to the sharks and then use the ship for piracy. Ashore, Mackenzie was the subject of a court of inquiry, which fully exonerated his conduct. At a subsequent court martial, convened at Mackenzie's request, he was acquitted of a charge of murder.

The execution of mutineer Richard Parker.

THE LOSS OF THE MIGHTIEST WARSHIP IN THE WORLD

Vasa was built in the 1620s for the new naval fleet of Sweden's King Gustavus Adolphus, one of the country's ablest and most successful military rulers. The first in a projected series of five great warships, *Vasa* was to be the mightiest in the world, armed with 64 guns on two gundecks, a broadside of nearly half a ton. Her cost had been 100,000 *dalers*, equivalent to the value of 10 per cent of the country's annual harvest.

On 10 August 1628 she was ready for her maiden voyage to the naval station at Alvsnabben, some 110 km around the coast, to pick up 300 soldiers before continuing to Poland, her final destination. Thousands of spectators crowded the vantage points in Stockholm's harbour, including foreign ambassadors, some of whom were no doubt spies of the king's enemies. *Vasa* was a magnificent sight, with hundreds of extravagant carvings and gold, green, red and blue paintwork. A flotilla of small boats gathered to see her on her way.

The day was calm and there was just a light breeze from the southwest. She was towed along the waterfront to the southern side of the harbour, where the sails were set, and she made way to the east. The gunports were open and the guns fired a salute.

As she left the harbour she was shielded by the cliffs, and light winds hardly filled her sails. Once the headland had been passed the wind freshened and she heeled to port. The sheets were cast off and *Vasa* righted herself. Then another gust came, again forcing her over. This time water poured in through the lower gunports and the glorious and mighty warship heeled further, then foundered, just 90 m from shore.

Survivors clung to debris and nearby boats raced to their aid. Of the 150 people on board, between 30 and 50 are believed to have perished, among them the helmsman. He had stayed at his post, where he would be found by archaeologists 333 years later.

After the disaster the captain of *Vasa* was arrested. The king was waging war in Poland at the time, and it took two weeks for him to learn of the disaster. He put it down to 'imprudence and negligence' and angrily demanded that the guilty parties be punished. At an official inquest held at Stockholm's royal castle all those who might have been responsible were called to account, but no one could be punished without awkward consequences, so the solution was to render no verdict at all.

In 1956 the wreck was found and discovered to be in an amazing state of preservation, and she was raised in 1961. Now housed in the purpose-built Vasa Museum in Stockholm, she is an international tourist attraction and provides a unique record of life aboard a seventeenth-century warship.

> **HIGH AND DRY** – stranded, without resources or support. DERIVATION: a beached ship or one up on blocks in the yard for repair or storage was said to be high and dry. For sailors, seeing their ship in effect out of its natural element, the sea, has a disturbing effect.

SWAMPED, DISMASTED AND ADRIFT

Polly, a brig of 118 metric tons, left Boston, Massachusetts, in December 1811 bound for Santa Cruz in the West Indies with a cargo of timber and salted meat for plantation slaves. Aboard was Captain William Cazuneau, the mate, four seamen, a cook and two passengers, a Mr J.S. Hunt and his female slave.

A week away from their destination they encountered a hurricane which forced the little ship over on her beam-ends. In desperation the crew clung to the rigging, which lay in an almost horizontal position. The captain ordered the masts to be cut away and the ship regained an even keel. She had taken a great deal of water on board, but the timber cargo kept her afloat. Mr Hunt and the young girl had been lost overboard.

When the storm blew itself out the crew managed to get hold of some casks of the salt meat, which they ate raw until the cook was able to get a makeshift stove going on deck. They supplemented this with fish and a few barnacles scraped off the hull. When their water ran out they devised a method of distilling seawater using an old iron tea kettle and the barrel of the captain's pistol as a tube attached to the spout.

Helpless, they drifted into the open Atlantic. Many distant sails were sighted, but as *Polly* was so low lying and her mast was gone she was not seen. One by one most of the crew succumbed to the extreme conditions and died. The survivors resorted to cannibalism of one of their fellow sailors, pickling part of his remains to preserve it for later consumption.

Eventually they were rescued 3,500 km west of Morocco by a British vessel. *Polly* had been adrift in the Atlantic for six months and had been borne over 3,200 km. Only two survived the ordeal, Captain Cazuneau and a seaman.

THE BARBARY TERROR

Pirates from the Barbary Coast of North Africa pillaged the length of the Mediterranean and north along Europe's Atlantic coastline for centuries. In the relatively calm waters of the Mediterranean merchant vessels could easily be overcome by the pirates' oar-powered galleys. The favoured tactic of the Barbary pirates was to creep up behind a ship, heave over grappling hooks and ropes and rapidly clamber aboard. The outcome of these encounters was almost invariably a swift victory for the pirates.

In April 1641 the Revd. Devereux Spratt joined the vessel *John Filmer* which was carrying 120 passengers across the Irish Sea to England. They had not even lost sight of land before they were all carried off by Barbary pirates as slaves. Spratt was lucky – he was ransomed after two years and was able to return home. Most of those snatched away suffered cruelly, chained to the oars in galleys, or forced into unremitting physical labour ashore, eventually meeting wretched deaths.

No Christian nation was immune. An American brig sailing for Cadiz in Spain in 1793 was about 110 km off the coast when a lookout spotted another brig flying the British flag. The master of the American vessel recognised by the cut of her sails that she was not British and assumed her to be a French privateer flying a false flag. Since the United States and France were not at war he felt he had nothing to fear, but he was sadly mistaken. In short order they were boarded by 100 heavily armed corsairs and taken prisoner, soon to find themselves incarcerated in Algiers.

Such was the extent of the Barbary terror that parish churches in Spain and Italy kept locked collection boxes marked 'for the poor slaves'. England even set aside an Algerian duty from customs income to finance redemptions. In 1646 Edward Casson headed a large-scale ransoming that freed 244 slaves, but these concerted efforts were rare – for most there was little hope.

The corsairs sometimes raided the British Isles. On 20 June 1631 the village of Baltimore on the southern coast of Ireland was attacked, and over 100 men, women and children were kidnapped and sold into slavery. Forays were made to southern English counties, too. In July 1625 corsairs wielding scimitars burst into a church in Mount's Bay, Cornwall, and dragged out 60 worshippers, who were shipped off to Morocco.

In the peak years of enslavement from 1530 to 1780 perhaps as many as one and a quarter million white Christians were taken to North Africa. In just one 20-year period, from 1622 to 1642, over 300 English ships and around 7,000 English subjects were captured by Barbary corsairs.

Private individuals, the church and the state were forced to pay exorbitant ransoms or fees to appease the demands of the Barbary pirates, and the cost in human suffering was huge. This terrible scourge of the seas finally ended in the early nineteenth century when Admiral Edward Pellew led a raid against Algiers, and the United States launched two major naval and land campaigns. The practice of capturing and enslaving Christians was finally crushed.

Barbary corsair.

MONEY FOR OLD ROPE – reward obtained for little effort. DERIVATION: the proceeds from selling old and frayed ship's ropes to shore-side traders was a perk of the boatswain. However, sometimes the rope was not so old and the offence of cappabar, misappropriation of government stores, was committed.

$\mathcal{T}$HE MYSTERIOUS ABANDONMENT OF *MARY CELESTE*

On 4 December 1872 a Canadian brigantine *Dei Gratia*, sailing from New York to the Mediterranean, encountered in mid Atlantic a ship whose abandonment at sea is a mystery to this day – she was *Mary Celeste*. No trace was ever found of her skipper Captain Briggs, the crew of seven or the captain's wife Sarah and her two-year-old daughter.

When the crew of *Dei Gratia* spotted *Mary Celeste* she was sailing erratically and they could see no one on deck. They boarded the vessel and found her in a disorderly but perfectly seaworthy condition, with no living soul anywhere aboard. There was sufficient food and water for several months, but the ship's boat was gone and the remains of the boat's painter hung over the stern. A cargo of 1,700 barrels of industrial alcohol was sound and unshifted, although when it was unloaded in Genoa nine barrels were found to be empty.

Sarah Briggs frequently accompanied her husband on ocean voyages, and in his cabin the boarding party found a picture of cosy Victorian domesticity, including a sewing machine and devotional literature. The last entry in the ship's logbook was 24 November. It noted the position as 160 km west of the Azores but made no reference to anything out of the ordinary.

Crewmen from *Dei Gratia* sailed *Mary Celeste* to Gibraltar, where they put in a claim for salvage. Frederick Flood, one of the officers in the Admiralty Court, suspected foul play after the discovery on board of an old sword with what appeared to be blood stains. (Later the marks were found to be rust.) It was suspected that there had been collusion between Captain Briggs and the master of *Dei Gratia* so that the salvage money could be claimed and then shared, but nothing was proved. In the end the court awarded a sum of money to the crew of *Dei Gratia*, but less than they were expecting.

There was no ready explanation for a seemingly sound and well-manned ship to have been deserted at sea. Various theories have been put forward such as a seaquake, poisoning from contaminated flour, collision with a giant squid, pirates and mutiny. However, the explanation that is given most credence today is that Captain Briggs opened the hold to ventilate it and there was a violent rush of fumes and vapour from escaped alcohol. Believing the ship was about to explode he ordered everyone into the lifeboat, and in the resulting panic it was not properly secured to the ship. As a result they drifted away, helpless, and either their boat foundered or they all died from hunger and exposure.

In 1884 Arthur Conan Doyle, writing under a pseudonym, published a story about a derelict ship he called *Marie Celeste*. His fictional tale, which recounted some of the actual events of *Mary Celeste,* captured the public interest.

eNGLAND'S PERFECT STORM

 Over 300 years ago, in late autumn, the British Isles was subjected to the most severe storm ever recorded there, the great tempest of 1703. Around 15,000 lives were lost, most of them in the 700 vessels sunk or damaged by the gales. Total damage was assessed at the equivalent today of half a billion pounds.

The Royal Navy lost 13 ships, many returning from helping the king of Spain fight the French. Some 1,500 seamen were drowned. A number of vessels even ended up in Sweden, Denmark, Norway and Holland. Sir

Cloudesley Shovell's HMS *Association* nearly foundered, but he cut his mainmast and his ship was blown from the Thames estuary to Sweden before she could make her way back safely to England.

One man had a remarkable tale to tell. When his ship HMS *Mary* was breaking up, Thomas Atkins saw Rear-Admiral Beaumont, who was aboard the vessel, grab a piece of timber, only to be washed off into the sea. A wave then carried Atkins from the sinking ship on to the deck of another vessel nearby, HMS *Stirling Castle,* which also soon began foundering. Another wave tossed him into one of *Stirling Castle*'s lifeboats. Atkins was the sole survivor of *Mary.*

When the storm struck in the West Country, right in its path was the newly constructed Eddystone Lighthouse. It was completely destroyed, along with its builder Henry Winstanley, who was making some additions to the structure at the time.

On the Thames, hundreds of ships were heaped together in the Pool of London, downstream from London Bridge. One ship at Whitstable in Kent was lifted from the sea by a gigantic surge and dropped some 230 m inland. Savage seas threw up spray which covered fields with a snow-like encrustation, making pastures inedible to grazing animals.

A young writer now known for his classic *Robinson Crusoe*, Daniel Defoe, published his first book, *The Storm*, the following year. He maintained that the destruction of the sovereign fleet was a punishment for their poor performance against the enemy.

Winstanley's Eddystone Lighthouse.

FURNACE AFLOAT

On 3 May 1866 in the middle of the Pacific Ocean, an accident occurred aboard what had been one of the fastest ships in the world, the American clipper ship *Hornet*. Deep in the hold first mate Sam Hardy and two hands spilt some varnish as they prepared to fill a can from a barrel of the liquid. They should have carried it on deck before decanting such an inflammable material, but they took a short cut – and they were carrying an open lantern. In seconds the varnish caught fire. A nearby wooden sail locker burst into flames and suddenly the entire area between decks was ablaze. The ship was carrying a cargo of 20,000 gallons of kerosene and 6,000 boxes of candles.

On deck, the fire spread rapidly – canvas blazed up and pitch boiled between the seams of the deck timbers. Frantic attempts were made to control the conflagration, but there was little time to do anything other than abandon ship.

Grabbing what they could, the 29 crew and officers and two passengers clambered into the three ship's boats and rowed to a safe distance. They had barely ten days' rations, but they felt sure that a ship would come to their rescue on seeing the great clouds of black smoke rolling up into the sky.

At 5 a.m. on 4 May the fire finally ate through the hull and *Hornet* plunged bow first into the deep. It would be six weeks and 6,900 km before the survivors reached Hawaii and safety. They were stalked by sharks, swordfish and waterspouts, desiccated by heat and thirst, and maddened and weakened by starvation. Of the 31 who had set out, only 15 survived.

A young reporter called Samuel Langhorne Clemens happened to be in Hawaii at the time. His articles about the tragedy of *Hornet* were printed worldwide and made his reputation. We know him today as Mark Twain.

> AT A STAND – taken by surprise and unsure of what to do next. DERIVATION: a vessel was said to be 'all standing' when she was fully equipped, or with all sails set. She could be 'brought up all standing' if, for example, under full sail she touched on a sandbank and shuddered to a stop.

A MELANCHOLY FATE

Lutine was originally a 26-gun frigate of the French Royal Navy, launched in Toulon in 1779 as *La Lutine*. Some years later, during the French Revolution, she was one of a dozen ships delivered to Admiral Hood by loyalists to prevent their use by Bonaparte, and in 1793 the vessel was commissioned into the Royal Navy under the name of HMS *Lutine*.

She was mainly used for convoy escort work, piloting larger transports through the treacherous waters off the coast of Holland. In October 1799 she was tasked to carry over £1 million in gold bullion and coin from England to Germany. The bullion was intended to fund German banks threatened with a stock market crash, the coin to pay troops fighting in Holland.

Lutine left English waters in the early morning of 9 October 1799 under the command of Captain Lancelot Skynner. Later that day she encountered a heavy northwesterly gale off the Dutch coast and struck on a sandbank. With a fierce tide coming in it was impossible for local boats to go to her aid, and by daybreak the next morning *Lutine* was smashed to pieces. Out of some 240 crew aboard, just one survived.

The loss of the ship was reported to the Admiralty by the commander of the local British squadron: 'It is with extreme pain that I have to state to you the melancholy fate of HMS *Lutine*...'

The cargo was insured by Lloyd's underwriters, who paid the claim in full, but ownership of the treasure that went down with the ship was disputed between the Dutch and the English. Several attempts over the years were made to retrieve some of the treasure, but much remains in Neptune's Realm.

The Lutine Bell

The ship's bell, recovered in 1858, took on a unique role and has hung in four successive Lloyd's Underwriting Rooms. For many years whenever a vessel became overdue underwriters involved in insuring the vessel would ask a specialist broker to reinsure some of their liability in the light of the possibility of the ship becoming a total loss. When reliable information about the vessel became available, the bell was rung once for bad news – such as total loss – or twice for a safe arrival or positive sighting. This ensured that all brokers and underwriters with an interest in the risk became aware of the news simultaneously.

The ringing of the Lutine Bell is now restricted principally to ceremonial occasions.

HMS Lutine.

So NEAR, YET SO FAR

Early on the morning of 23 November 1797 the Royal Navy frigate HMS *Tribune* made landfall in the approaches to the harbour at Halifax, Nova Scotia. She was part of a convoy escort for merchant vessels from England bound for Canada but had become separated from the other ships in heavy weather out in the Atlantic. Her captain proposed that they wait until a pilot could come aboard, but the master assured him that this was not necessary as he knew the harbour well.

Not long afterwards soldiers of the 7th Fusiliers stationed at York Redoubt watched with disbelief as *Tribune* careered on to Thrumcap Shoal less than 2 km from the harbour mouth. From their position on top of the high bluffs they relayed *Tribune*'s distress signals to the dockyard. Boats put out from the harbour to go to the assistance of the stranded vessel, but strong winds forced them back.

In an effort to lighten the ship, her starboard guns were manhandled over the side. That evening *Tribune* floated off the shoal but she had lost her rudder and there was 2 m of water in the hold. The pumps were worked furiously, and at first they seemed to be succeeding, but as the storm worsened the sea flooded in. The raging winds drove the ship inexorably towards the craggy shore on the other side of the harbour, then suddenly she lurched and sank in shallow water just off the entrance to Herring Cove.

Nearly 250 sailors found themselves struggling in the icy waves. Those who tried to swim to shore were smashed against the rocks. Eventually around 100 survivors managed to climb into the rigging, which protruded above the waves, but as night wore on many fell off through exhaustion and were swept away in the frigid waters.

All night people on shore at Herring Cove kept a grim vigil by the light of bonfires. They were so close to the wreck that they could hear the hopeless cries of the weakening survivors, but could no nothing.

The following morning a 13-year-old boy named Joe Cracker set out from the shore in a small skiff and with great courage and skill managed to bring it to the wreck and take off two men. His example inspired others, and shortly afterwards the rest were rescued, but just 12 out of 250 of the ship's company had survived.

Edward, Duke of Kent, then resident in Halifax, personally thanked Cracker for his courage and asked him to name a reward. The boy requested a pair of warm corduroy breeches.

The location of the tragic sinking was named Tribune Head. A plaque at the headland at Herring Cove reads: 'In memory of the heroism of Joe Cracker the fisher lad of 13 years who was the first to rescue survivors from the wreck of HMS *Tribune*.'

Eighteenth-century map of Chebucto Harbour and Halifax.

*T*HE FUNERAL THAT BURIED A FLEET

In 1566 in the Baltic Sea a fleet of the Swedish navy met a fleet of ships from Denmark and Lübeck in a battle during which a Danish commander was killed by a cannonball. A storm was brewing and, as was the custom, the opposing forces ceased fire and went their separate ways. The Swedish fleet disappeared into the Stockholm archipelago and the Danish-Lübeck forces formed a funeral procession and set course for the nearest Danish territory, the island of Gotland. The Lübeckians had wanted to go initially to Danzig, where their battle-scarred ships could be repaired, but the Danes insisted that the dead must be buried first.

Arriving off the Gotland port of Visby, Jens Truidson, the Danish Vice-Admiral commanding the fleet, was advised by harbour authorities not to anchor in the roadstead as it was a foul ground, and in anything other than a flat calm there was a great risk of anchors dragging. But the admiral, determined on honouring their dead, ignored the warning and ordered his 39 ships to anchor. They then began the gruesome business of ferrying the dead ashore.

The following day a burial service was held in Visby Cathedral, and the squadron prepared to leave the next morning. The weather was calm initially, but then the sky went a strange colour and the sea seemed to shimmer beneath the ships. That night Visby was hit by a terrible storm that lasted for six hours.

Anchors were ripped from the seabed and cables snapped. The unwieldy ships of the Danish-Lübeck fleet collided with each other or were dashed to pieces on the jagged shoreline as they tried to sail away.

At daybreak the beach was covered with debris and dead bodies. More than one-third of the fleet was gone: 15 ships had sunk and the storm had claimed between 5,000 and 7,000 lives. (To put this into perspective, the population of Stockholm at the time was 9,000.) Among the dead were Admiral Truidson and his wife, two other admirals and the mayor of Lübeck; their remains were buried in Visby Cathedral. It was a hot summer and the people of Visby, fearing an epidemic could break out, hastily buried the rest of the dead in mass graves.

A Lübecker of 1540.

> BROUGHT UP SHORT – forced to a standstill by a
> sudden reversal of fortune. DERIVATION: a vessel under
> way was said to be brought up short if she was forced to
> shudder to an emergency stop by dropping her anchors, for
> example on unexpectedly sighting a coast looming through a
> thick fog.

$\mathcal{A}$ DOCKYARD'S NIGHTMARE

With so many combustibles around, fire was an ever-present danger in a dockyard. In 1774 Portsmouth dockyard, Britain's biggest at that time, had already suffered two serious conflagrations in living memory.

In the late afternoon of 7 December fire broke out in the rope house. All but two of the workers had left the building by then, but once the alarm was raised hundreds of men quickly arrived on the scene, well aware that should a fire take hold there would be huge destruction. In addition to all the hemp, timbers, workshops and tools there were five ships in dry dock for repairs and a number of warships on slips in various stages of construction. Fortunately, although the rope house was destroyed, the fire was contained.

Initially the blaze was thought to have been an accident, but the evidence pointed to arson and a hunt began for the perpetrator. Suspicion fell on a man who was known as John the Painter, and an advertisement was placed in newspapers offering a reward for his apprehension.

Somewhat of a social misfit, John the Painter's real name was James Hill, alias Hinde, alias Aitken. He had previously fled overseas to the American colonies to avoid arrest for a number of crimes. There he had consorted with political revolutionaries and come up with the wild plan of setting fire to England's dockyards.

On 10 March 1775 a shackled Hill was transported to the dockyard, the scene of his crime. A public gallows had been erected around the mizzenmast of HMS *Arethusa*. Before he died, Hill apologised for his actions and exhorted the authorities to exercise 'great care and strict vigilance' at the dockyards in future. A crowd of 20,000 watched his execution, and then the lifeless body was placed in a gibbet and rowed across the harbour entrance to Blockhouse Point and suspended there for all to see.

The fate of the remains of Jack the Painter, as he became known posthumously, is uncertain. Rumour has it that sailors took down the skeleton and used it to pay an ale-house debt. A mummified finger supposedly cut from his hand was used as a tobacco stopper for many years in Portsmouth.

> HAND OVER FIST – financial gain due to a rapid ascent up the ladder of success. DERIVATION: a skilled seaman developed great speed and agility for climbing aloft into the rigging. This involved considerable upper body strength, with the free hand passing over the fist in which the rope was clenched as he swarmed up the rigging.

TOLL FOR THE BRAVE

HMS *Royal George* was a first-rate of 100 guns that had served in many battles including the American War of Independence. Flagship of Rear Admiral Richard Kempenfelt, and captained by Martin Waghorn, she was anchored at Spithead on 29 August 1782. Almost the entire crew were on board, together with many visiting women and children as well as dockyard craftsmen.

At 7 a.m. in the morning stores tenders arrived carrying dockyard plumbers and carpenters to install a cistern pipe to provide water for washing the decks. In order for this to be done the ship needed to be heeled over so that a hole could be bored into the side. The lower deck larboard guns were run out and the starboard guns pulled back inboard. Unfortunately this did not give a sufficient heel for the plumbers and shipwrights to work, so the upper deck guns and some of those on the middle deck were repositioned.

After breakfast Captain Waghorn was on the upper deck when the carpenter announced that the ship appeared to be settling in the water. Orders were given to move the guns to right the ship, but suddenly she sank so quickly that over 900 people perished, including the admiral.

Around 300 survived, among them Captain Waghorn. Many of those who lost their lives in the wreck were laid to rest in the old burial grounds of Haslar Hospital at Gosport, possibly including the remains of Kempenfelt himself.

The cause of the tragedy was never established. One theory was that the hull was so rotten that it gave way while being worked on; another possible reason put forward was that the carpenter introduced too much heeling, bringing her gunports below water. At the subsequent court martial evidence supported both arguments but failed to rule out either.

The tragedy inspired the poet William Cowper to write a lament, entitled 'Toll for the Brave':

> Brave Kempenfelt is gone
> His last sea fight is fought
> His work of glory done
> It was not in the battle
> No tempest gave the shock
> She sprang no fatal leak
> She ran upon no rock
> His sword was in his sheath
> His fingers held the pen
> When Kempenfelt went down
> With twice four hundred men.

SHIPWRECK STRAIT

Bass Strait, separating mainland Australia from Tasmania, is among the most lethal stretches of water in the world, twice as rough as the English Channel. The infamous strait has claimed hundreds of ships and more than 1,000 lives, but many ship captains risked the dangerous passage in order to shorten by weeks their voyage time from the west.

Sydney Cove was wrecked on Preservation Island in Bass Strait on 28 February 1797. A party of 17 men led by first mate Hugh Thompson set off in the ship's longboat, heading for Port Jackson, 645 km away; the rest of the crew, including the captain, set up a rough shelter ashore to await rescue. After a few days at sea Thompson's boat was wrecked and the seamen found themselves cast ashore in a totally unknown land with few provisions. Their only hope was to try to reach Port Jackson some 600 km away by foot, following the coast. Finally, in May the last three survivors, near death, managed to signal an offshore fishing boat which took them to Sydney. Two ships were dispatched to collect the men remaining on Preservation Island, but on their return journey one of these vessels was wrecked with the loss of the crew and eight of the *Sydney Cove* survivors.

The female convict ship *Neva* sailed from Cork, Ireland, on 8 January 1835 bound for the penal colony of Sydney. Four months later she entered Bass Strait with a gale on her port quarter. In the early hours of 14 May the dreaded cry rang out, 'Breakers ahead!' She struck rocks and her rudder was carried away, then her bow hit the main reef and she swung broadside on. Heavy seas broke over the ship. The straining of the hull caused prison stanchions to give way and the terrified female prisoners and children swarmed on deck. Some of them were washed overboard; others broke into the rum stowage and drank themselves insensible. Four hours after striking the rocks the ship broke up and sank. Of the 240 who had left Cork only 15 survived.

Cataraqui was a barque transporting assisted emigrants from England to Port Phillip (present-day Melbourne) in the colony of Victoria. She set sail under the command of Captain Christopher Finlay on 20 April 1845 with 376 emigrants and 41 crew. As the vessel entered Bass Strait after six long months at sea, those on board were eagerly looking forward to making land, having been tossed about by a storm for several days. Suddenly, the ship struck on rocks and quickly sank. Eight crew and one emigrant managed to reach shore by clinging to wreckage. Daylight presented the horrible scene of hundreds of bodies strewn along about 3 km of beach. The castaways were stranded for five weeks, living with a party of seal hunters, before they were rescued by a cutter and taken to Melbourne. The loss of *Cataraqui* is Australia's worst peacetime sea disaster.

In 1871 Loch Leven *became another victim of Bass Strait.*

*T*HE MOTHER OF ALL SHIP EXPLOSIONS

The French flagship *L'Orient* was a three-deck floating fortress of 4,500 metric tons and with a crew of 1,100. At the Battle of the Nile she first came under attack from the guns of HMS *Bellerophon*, then HMS *Alexander* and HMS *Swiftsure* continued a savage bombardment.

Aboard the flagship Vice-Admiral Brueys showed the utmost personal courage. Already suffering from a head wound, he was hit by a cannonball that blew off both his legs. Refusing to go below, he had a tourniquet bound around the stumps and, propped up in a chair on the quarterdeck, he continued to issue orders. Brueys was spared the final ignominy of seeing his ship destroyed when a roundshot took off his head.

By about 9 p.m. the ship was ablaze aft, and fire spread up the rigging and mast like a gigantic torch illuminating the battle. The French gunners courageously continued firing, although they must have known their fate. Ships tried to move away to what they hoped would be a safe distance. At about 10 p.m. the fire reached the magazine and *L'Orient* exploded in an incredible spectacle, with blazing parts of the ship hurled hundreds of metres into the air.

After the explosion both sides fell into a stunned silence for about ten minutes and an eerie light pervaded the scene. The noise had been heard over 30 km away. The whole of Aboukir Bay seemed covered with mangled, wounded, scorched bodies. Of *L'Orient*'s crew only 100 or so survived by swimming from the blazing wreck; they were plucked from the sea by British sailors.

All the while Napoleon Bonaparte and his military staff were grimly watching the battle from a tower in Alexandria, 14 km away.

According to legend, Luc, the young son of Commodore Casa Bianca, the captain of *L'Orient,* obediently stayed at his post waiting for his father's order to leave the ship – an order that never came, as he was lying unconscious below deck.

Felicia Hemans would later write the poignant verse:

> The boy stood on the burning deck
> Whence all but he had fled;
> The flame that lit the battle's wreck
> Shone round him o'er the dead...

Who The Deuce Are You, Sir?

In the aftermath of the explosion a survivor appeared on the quarterdeck of *Swiftsure*, naked except for a cocked hat. 'Who the deuce are you, sir?' snapped Captain Hallowell. 'Je suis de *L'Orient*, monsieur,' came the response. He was Lieutenant Berthelot, who had managed to escape the flames by leaping into the sea. He had removed his heavy clothes before doing so and then realised that without them he would not be recognised as an officer. Hastily climbing back aboard, he fought his way back to where he had left his clothes, retrieved his hat and then jumped overboard again.

L'Orient *explodes at the Battle of the Nile.*

Stockwin's Top 25
MUSEUMS &
HISTORIC SHIPS

AUSTRALIA

Australian National Maritime Museum
2 Murray Street
Darling Harbour
Sydney
New South Wales
Telephone: +61 2 9298 3777
Open: daily except Christmas Day

The words of the country's national anthem celebrate 'a land girt by sea' and Australians have always had a special connection with the water. Located on the largest natural harbour in the world, the Australian National Maritime Museum has seven main galleries of permanent exhibitions, including the early navigators who mapped the great continent and the long sea voyages of the first settlers. Of special significance in the wonderful fleet of ships and boats maintained by the museum is the replica of James Cook's *Endeavour*. This vessel returned to Sydney in 2005 having completed 11 years of voyaging around the world and from time to time still takes to the water to bring alive eighteenth-century square-rig seamanship.

http://www.anmm.gov.au/site/page.cfm

BERMUDA

Bermuda Maritime Museum
The Keep
Royal Naval Dockyard
Sandys Parish
Telephone: 1-441-234-1418
Open: daily except Christmas Day

Bermuda's largest fort, the Keep, was originally constructed to defend the Royal Naval Dockyard. Today this 2.5-hectare fortress is home to the Bermuda Maritime Museum, which chronicles the island's maritime history from the early sixteenth century. The complex comprises seven bastions and eight buildings filled with artefacts and historic exhibits. On the lower grounds, in the cavernous Queen's Exhibition hall, 4,860 kegs of gunpowder were once stored and the building's floor is made of non-sparking bitumen. The crown jewel of the museum is the Commissioner's House, which was completed in 1827. It was the world's first cast-iron building; its girders, red brick and flagstones were shipped from England in the 1820s, while its 1-m thick walls consist of limestone quarried from the dockyard.

http://www.bmm.bm/

CANADA

The Maritime Museum of the Atlantic
1675 Lower Water Street
Halifax
Nova Scotia
Telephone: (902) 424-7490
Open: daily in the summer months, closed for major public holidays and on Mondays in winter

This is the oldest and largest maritime museum in Canada. After a number of temporary locations the museum was established on the site of the historic William Robertson & Son Ship Chandlery and A.M. Smith and Co. Properties on the Halifax waterfront. Among this museum's permanent exhibitions is the Days of Sail Gallery with ship models, images, charts and a sailmaker's loft. A Royal Navy dockyard was founded in Halifax in 1758, and the museum's Navy Gallery bears witness to its presence with such items as artefacts from the famous encounter nearby between *Shannon* and *Chesapeake*. Among the museum's more modern items is its large collection of *Titanic* memorabilia.

http://museum.gov.ns.ca/mma/index.html

FRANCE

Musée de la Marine
Palais de Chaillot
17, place du Trocadéro
75116 Paris
Telephone: 33 (0)1 53 65 69 45
Open: daily except Tuesday and national holidays

The museum traces its origins back to 1748 when Louis Henri du Monceau, general inspector of France's navy, asked King Louis XV whether he would be prepared to donate his personal ship and shipyard-machinery models for a collection to be exhibited in the Louvre. Now housed in the Palais de Chaillot, a stone's throw from the Eiffel Tower, the museum's highlights include its ship model collection and Napoleon's state barge, as well as paintings of naval battles, uniforms and navigational instruments. Annexes at Brest, Port-Louis, Rochefort and Toulon also celebrate France's truly rich seafaring heritage with specialist collections.

http://www.musee-marine.fr/index.php?lg=en&nav=1&flash=1

HOLLAND

The National Maritime Museum
Kattenburgerplein 1
Amsterdam

The National Maritime Museum has a superb collection telling the story of the maritime heritage of the Netherlands. However, the museum is currently closed for a major renovation of the 300-year-old building which houses the exhibits. The *Amsterdam*, a replica of an eighteenth-century Dutch Indiaman that was moored outside the museum, is still open to the public but has been moved until the refurbishment of the museum is complete.

Amsterdam – temporary site:
Science center NEMO
Oosterdok 2
1011 VX Amsterdam
Open: Tuesday to Sunday, plus Monday during school holidays and peak season.
Closed on public holidays
http://www.scheepvaartmuseum.nl/english

HONG KONG

The Hong Kong Maritime Museum
G/F Murray House
Stanley Plaza
Telephone: +852 2813 2322
Open: daily except Mondays and Chinese New Year

One of Asia's newest institutional celebrations of the history and culture of the sea, the Hong Kong Maritime Museum was opened in 2005. The focus of the museum is how China, Asia and the West have interacted in the development of boats, ships, maritime exploration and trade, and naval warfare. The exhibits are displayed in two main areas – the Ancient Gallery and the Modern Gallery, with ship models, paintings, ceramics, trade goods and ship manifests. A model of a 2,000-year-old boat made of pottery from the Han Dynasty is one of the many priceless treasures on display.

www.hkmaritimemuseum.org

ITALY

Museo Storico Navale
Castello, 2148
30100
Venice
Telephone: 0415200276
Open: Monday to Saturday

At the height of Venice's naval power in the fifteenth century, the Arsenale, the focus of the republic's military operations, occupied one-fifth of the area of the city and employed over 16,000 workers who turned out vessel after vessel, both for commercial and military use, in massive assembly lines. The Museo Storico Navale, situated close to the Arsenale, is a vast museum devoted to the maritime achievements of the Venetian republic and story of the Italian navy. The highlight of the model ships exhibition is a lavish model of the *Bucintoro*, the golden ceremonial barge of the ruler of Venice, the doge. The museum's art treasures include a sixteenth-century frieze that depicts Venice's famous victory against the Ottoman empire at the Battle of Lepanto in 1572.

http://www2.regione.veneto.it/cultura/musei/inglese/pag462e.htm

MALTA

The Maritime Museum of Malta
Vittoriosa
Grand Harbour
Telephone: +356 2295 4000, 2295 4300
Open: daily except major public holidays

Housed in the former British Naval Bakery, the museum was built over the site of the slipway where the Knights of St John, who ruled Malta for nearly three centuries, launched their galleys. The bakery remained part of the naval establishment up until the closure of the British base in 1979. The museum celebrates the island's rich maritime history and the broader Mediterranean maritime context. A prized exhibit is a model of the French ship of the line *Bucentaure*, made by captive French sailors during the Napoleonic wars. Maltese sea crafts are well represented, as are uniforms, weapons and artefacts from the Royal Navy's days in Malta.

http://www.visitmalta.com/the-maritime-museum

PORTUGAL

Museu de Marinha
Praça do Império
1400-206
Lisbon
Telephone: +351 – 21 – 362 00 10
Open: daily except Monday. Closed on national holidays

The treasures of the museum are displayed in themed rooms. In the entrance hall is a planisphere that celebrates the boldness and daring of the Portuguese explorers of the fifteenth century. The museum has a very fine collection of astrolabes. One poignant artefact in the museum is a figure of the archangel Raphael, which Paulo da Gama carried in his ship *Sao Rafael* in the famous voyage of 1497. When his ship was wrecked he managed to save the archangel, but he died shortly afterwards. After that his brother Vasco da Gama kept the figure always by his side.

http://www.museumarinha.pt/museu/ENG/Homepage/index.aspx

SPAIN

Maritime Museum of Barcelona
Av. de les Drassanes s/n
08001 Barcelona
Telephone: 933 429 920
Open: daily except major public holidays

Fittingly sited opposite a statue of Christopher Columbus, the Maritime Museum of Barcelona is located in the royal arsenals that date from the fourteenth century and are the most complete medieval dockyards in the world. The museum celebrates not just Spain's extensive seafaring heritage but that of the Mediterranean as a whole. Of note is 'The Great Adventure of the Sea', an interactive exhibition that is a homage to Catalonia's maritime history. There is also a unique collection of votive paintings by sailors, and a wide range of models, figureheads and maritime paintings.

http://www.mmb.cat/default.asp?idApartado=97&idIdioma=3

SWEDEN

Vasa Museum
Galärvarvsvägen 14
Stockholm
Telephone: +46-8-519 558 10
Open: daily, closed over Christmas

Vasa, the only remaining intact seventeenth-century ship in the world, was rediscovered on the seabed of Stockholm harbour in 1956 in a remarkable state of preservation. Excavation work went on until 1967 and she was put on public view in a specially constructed building in 1990. Visitors to the Vasa Museum are almost overwhelmed by their first sight of the ship, over 50 m long, illuminated in the soft light of the vast purpose-built ship's hall. The lower rig has been rebuilt complete with masts, stays and shrouds, just as the ship would have looked when set for winter in harbour. A superb 1:10 scale model recreates the glorious colours of her original livery and ornamentation.

http://www.vasamuseet.se/InEnglish/about.aspx

UNITED KINGDOM

National Maritime Museum of Great Britain
Romney Road
Greenwich
London SE10 9NF
Telephone: +44 (0)20 8312 6565
Opening hours: daily, closed over Christmas

Three sites – the Maritime Galleries (covering the sixteenth to the early twentieth centuries), the Royal Observatory and the Queen's House (showcasing a priceless art collection) – together constitute one museum dedicated to the sea, ships, time and the stars and their relationship with people. Among the most moving exhibits is the actual coat worn by Nelson at the Battle of Trafalgar, the bullet hole from the musket-ball which killed him clearly visible on the left shoulder. The National Maritime Museum is arguably the world's greatest maritime collection of paintings, prints, models, relics, manuscripts, instruments, weapons and charts.

http://www.nmm.ac.uk/

Chatham Historic Dockyard
Chatham
Kent ME4 4TZ
Telephone: +44 (0)1634 823807
Open: daily. Restricted hours or closed in November, December and January

The complex is set in 32 hectares. Down the centuries the great names of maritime history, Francis Drake, John Hawkins, Horatio Nelson and many others, have all sailed from here. This was the birthplace of many of the navy's most celebrated ships, including HMS *Victory*. One fascinating exhibition is 'Wooden Walls' which follows William Crockwell, an apprentice shipwright, on his first day at work on the 74-gun ship of the line HMS *Valiant*. He is introduced to many of the different trades involved in building the ship. The Ropery, with its 400-m long Double Ropehouse, is the only working traditional rope-walk from the age of sail to survive anywhere in the world. Chatham closed as a working dockyard in 1984 and was redeveloped as a historic dockyard celebrating four centuries of naval history. It is the most complete dockyard of the age of sail in existence.

http://www.chdt.org.uk/

Buckler's Hard
Beaulieu
Brockenhurst
Hampshire SO42 7XB
Telephone: 01590 616203
Open: daily except Christmas Day

A hard is a place where boats and ships are landed, the muddy bottom being covered with gravel or shingle. Buckler's Hard developed as a thriving shipbuilding village where warships for Nelson's navy were built, three of which took part in the Battle of Trafalgar. Nelson's favourite HMS *Agamemnon* was built at Buckler's Hard and launched in 1781. As well as fascinating information on how wooden ships were built and many superb ship models the museum has a fine collection of Nelson memora-bilia including his baby clothes made for him by citizens of his birthplace, Burnham Thorpe in Norfolk.

http://www.bucklershard.co.uk/ipus/bucklershard/index

Portsmouth Historic Dockyard

HM Naval Base
Portsmouth
Hampshire PO1 3LJ
Telephone: 023 9286 1512
Opening hours: daily, closed over Christmas

Unique in its combination of historic site, naval museum and famous ships (*Mary Rose*, HMS *Victory* and HMS *Warrior*), the dockyard draws huge crowds of visitors each year. Its origins go back to the twelfth century when Richard I ordered the construction of a dockyard in Portsmouth. The Royal Naval Museum has a very fine Sailing Navy Gallery, housed in a restored eighteenth-century storehouse. To go on board *Victory* and peep into Nelson's cabin, then to go and see the spot where he died on the orlop is to experience a moving connection with history.

http://www.historicdockyard.co.uk/

Cutty Sark

King William Walk
Greenwich
London SE10 9HT
Telephone: 020 8858 2698
Closed until 2010

Now in permanent berth in dry dock, this famed vessel has attracted over 15 million visitors. With her shapely hull, steeply raked bow and wondrous spread of sail, the clipper was arguably the most beautiful ship ever built. *Cutty Sark* travelled across the world sailing under both the Red Ensign and the Portuguese flag, visiting every major port through the course of her working life. She is the world's sole surviving extreme clipper and the only tea clipper still in existence. Currently undergoing conservation and preservation, she will reopen to the public in spring 2011. There are some facilities at the site for viewing the conservation work through a special observation dome.

www.cuttysark.org.uk

HMS *Trincomalee*

Hartlepool's Maritime Experience
Jackson Dock
Maritime Avenue
Hartlepool TS24 0XZ
Telephone: 01429 860077
Open: daily, closed over Christmas

Located within the Hartlepool Maritime Experience complex, this venerable historic ship is the oldest British fighting ship still afloat. She was built in Bombay in 1817 as a frigate, a fifth-rate ship of 46 guns. Later she was reduced to a sixth-rate and served all over the world from the Pacific to the Arctic Circle. In 1898 she was renamed *Foudroyant* and served as a training ship. Now she is fully restored with her original name.

http://www.hms-trincomalee.co.uk/

Docklands Museum
West India Quay
Canary Wharf
London E14 4AL
Telephone: 020 7001 9844
Open: daily, closed over Christmas

Housed in a Georgian warehouse that once stored imports of exotic spices, rum and cotton from all over the world, this museum explores the 2,000-year-old history of London's river and port – and the people who lived and worked there. During the eighteenth century there was a great increase in international trade, and by 1800 the number of ships entering the port had increased 400 per cent. One of the focuses of the museum's permanent exhibitions is the development of London's port and docks to cater to this rapid expansion.

http://www.museumindocklands.org.uk/English/

Golden Hinde
St Mary Overie Dock
Cathedral St
London SE1 9DE
Telephone: 020 7403 0123
Open: daily, but in case of closure for functions it is advisable to check before visiting

This is a full-sized reconstruction of the famous Tudor warship in which Sir Francis Drake circumnavigated the world in 1577–80. Queen Elizabeth I visited the galleon on Drake's return and decreed that the ship should be preserved at Deptford so that the general public could visit the ship and celebrate England's success. The original *Golden Hinde* therefore became Britain's first museum ship! This replica ship, now permanently berthed in London, has herself circumnavigated the globe.

http://www.goldenhinde.com/

Merseyside Maritime Museum
Albert Dock
Liverpool L3 4AQ
Telephone: 0151 478 4499
Opening hours: daily, closed over Christmas

Located in an old warehouse in Albert Dock, the museum celebrates the city's long-held seafaring traditions and particularly the importance of the merchant navy. The museum's exhibits reflect the city's role in the transatlantic slave trade and emigration. One of the jewels of the museum is its collection of ships in bottles made by

Jo Dashwood-Howard. Among the fine collection of ship models are 39 miniature ships made by French prisoners of war during the Napoleonic wars.
http://www.liverpoolmuseums.org.uk/maritime/

UNITED STATES

Nantucket Whaling Museum
15 Broad Street
Nantucket
Massachusetts
Telephone: 508 2281894
Open: check website for current details

Many people today look on whaling with revulsion, but in the past it was generally seen as a brave, romantic – and lucrative – enterprise. In the eighteenth and nine-teenth centuries Yankee whaling ships sailed the oceans of the world for years at a time, returning with oil for the lamps of America and Europe. The Nantucket Whaling Museum houses a fascinating record of the heyday of whaling, including ships' logs, a huge finback whale skeleton and scrimshaw.
http://www.nha.org/sites/index.html

The Museum of America and the Sea
Mystic Seaport
Connecticut
Telephone: 860 572 5315
Open: daily. Closed Mondays in the winter months and over Christmas

Located on the banks of the Mystic River, an area with centuries-old maritime tradi-tions, this foremost living history museum features a re-created nineteenth-century seafaring village, an impressive collection of sailing ships and boats (including the *Charles W. Morgan*, the world's last wooden whaleship) and a preservation shipyard where craftsmen keep alive old skills with the use of traditional methods and tools. As well, over the 15-hectare site, there are many formal exhibits and galleries plus a planetarium that demonstrates how seamen used the stars for navigation.
http://www.mysticseaport.org/

The Mariners' Museum
Newport News
Virginia
Telephone: (757) 596-2222
Open: daily, closed over Christmas

Over 5,600 square metres of gallery space showcase all manner of splendid sea artefacts. The collection of 1,200 nautical navigation instruments includes such treasures as a mid-seventeenth-century silver astrolabe and a marine barometer thought to have been on Cook's voyages. Among the other permanent exhibitions is 'The Age

of Exploration', which chronicles the developments in shipbuilding, ocean navigation and cartography that made possible the voyages of the period between the fifteenth
and eighteenth centuries. A perennial favourite is the ship model collection of August
F. Crabtree.

>   http://www.mariner.org/index.php?oatsad=29

USS *Constitution*
Building 5, Charlestown Navy Yard
Charlestown
Massachusetts
Telephone: (617) 242 – 5670
Open: see website for current details

Affectionately known as 'Old Ironsides', she's the oldest warship afloat still in commission and America's 'Ship of State'. The vessel was launched on 21 October 1797 from
a shipyard a stone's throw from her current berth just across the Charles River from
Boston. USS *Constitution* was one of six frigates built to form the genesis of the US
Navy. In the War of 1812 in an encounter with HMS *Guerriere* a cannonball bounced
off her thick hull, at which a sailor reportedly shouted, 'Huzzah! Her sides are made
of iron!' She is still crewed, maintained and sailed by the US Navy.

>   http://www.history.navy.mil/USSconstitution/index.html

Maritime Museum of San Diego
1492 North Harbor Drive
San Diego
California
Telephone: 619-234-9153
Open: daily

This maritime museum features one of the finest collections of historic ships in
the world including the world's oldest active ship, *Star of India*. An 1863 barque,
she now sails at least once a year. You can also see HMS *Surprise*, the replica of
an eighteenth-century Royal Navy frigate that featured in the film *Master and
Commander*. The museum's permanent collection is presented in five galleries
representing major themes of maritime history.

>   http://www.sdmaritime.com/

Golden Age of Sail
SOME KEY DATES

Sail opens up the world *Square-rigged ships make heroic open-ocean voyages practical*

1405	China's great exploration fleet sets sail
1492	Columbus reaches America
1519	Magellan captains the first voyage around the world
1545	Henry VIII sees *Mary Rose*, the first broadside-equipped warship, sink before his eyes
1588	Francis Drake and others defeat the Spanish Armada

Race for Empire *Nations clash as they discover and colonise the world*

1600s	Dutch, French and English vie for empire
1650s–1750s	dark age of pirates
1696	work begins on the first open-sea lighthouse, at Eddystone Rock
1700s	science and seamanship flourish: reliable charts, sextant, chronometer
1758	HMS *Victory* built
1766–79	Captain Cook's three epic voyages; now the world is known

Climax of Age of Sail *The struggle to dominate the seas*

1780s	sea trade patterns criss-cross the globe
1793–1815	Revolutionary and Napoleonic Wars; Britain against France
1800s	design of ships becomes scientific
1805	Nelson at Trafalgar
1815	Napoleon goes into exile

Sunset of Age of Sail *Steam and brute force; end of an era*

1821	first steam tug for Royal Navy
1838	*Great Western* inaugurates regular Atlantic crossings
1850–1865	heyday of the clipper ship
1866	the Great Tea Race
1869	*Cutty Sark* launched
1900s	last Royal Navy ships under square-rig
1960s	final mercantile ocean voyages under sail

Size Matters

There were hundreds of ship types in the Golden Age of Sail, ranging from the smugglers' *abari* to the corsairs' *xebec*. Here are the vital statistics of some of history's famous wooden ships, along with three of today's grandest vessels for comparison.

Name	Tons	Length	Crew
Nina the smallest of Columbus's famous trio, a caravel	54 metric tons	15 m	27
Black Joke anti-slavery poacher-turned-gamekeeper	67 metric tons	17 m	35
Bluenose iconic Canadian fishing schooner	89 metric tons	34 m	30
Victoria Spanish carrack, first ship to circumnavigate the world	106 metric tons	19 m	280
Windsor Castle gallant Falmouth packet ship	154 metric tons	23 m	28
Speedy Cochrane's daring brig-sloop	189 metric tons	24 m	54
Essex whaleship that inspired *Moby Dick*	216 metric tons	27 m	22
Queen Anne's Revenge pirate Blackbeard's famous flagship	272 metric tons	32 m	180

Revenge Grenville's plucky fifteenth-century galleon	363 metric tons	40 m	153
Mary Rose Henry VIII's war carrack	635 metric tons	38 m	415
Vasa Swedish ship of the line that sank on her maiden voyage	1,200 metric tons	69 m	445
Cutty Sark the clipper that overtook a steamship	1,905 metric tons	65 m	30
USS *Constitution* famous early American frigate	1,996 metric tons	62 m	475
Zheng He's treasure-ship Chinese nine-masted junk	2,449 metric tons	127 m	2,500
HMS *Victory* most famous wooden wall	3,175 metric tons	69 m	850
Santissima Trinidad giant Spanish ship of the line	4,490 metric tons	61 m	1,050
Queen Mary beloved ocean liner	81,961 metric tons	311 m	1,101
USS *George H.W. Bush* American nuclear aircraft carrier	88,000 metric tons	333 m	5,000
Knock Nevis Dubai-based super-tanker	564,763 metric tons	458 m	39

Glossary

aquatint	type of etching
Articles of War	the code of law under which the Royal Navy operates and which all must obey
ash-man	waste collector
backstay	rope steadying a mast in opposition to the pressure of the sails
ballast	weight in the lowest part of the ship to balance the wind blowing on the sails, usually beach shingle
barricoe	a small keg – pronounced 'breaker'
beakhead	like the beak of a bird, the carved fore part of the bows with its deck
beam-ends	the beam of a ship is its extremity across; she would be on her beam-ends if the wind bore down too forcefully on one side
bilboes	shackles on a long iron bar acting as leg irons; equivalent to the stocks on land
binnacle	housing for the compass with provision for night-time illumination and later the magnetically corrective Flinders bar
blockade	prevention of ships from entering or leaving harbour
boarding party	group of seamen sent to attack, seize or search a vessel
boom end	a boom spreads the lower edge of the sail, the end protrudes over the stern
bowsprit	long spar projecting over the bow to carry the headsails
brig	a two-masted vessel, square-sailed on both masts
brig-sloop	brig captained by a commander
broadside	simultaneous firing of the artillery on one side of a ship, also a side of the ship as opposed to the bows or stern
buccaneer	pirate rover of Spanish Main, from *boucan*, their dried meat ration
bulkhead	vertical partition between decks
bulwark	raised woodwork running along the sides of a vessel above the level of the deck
butcher's bill	casualties sustained during a battle
capstan	a mechanical device for lifting the anchor, and other heavy items
cathead	wooden support projecting from the bow for swinging in the anchor
chaise	type of fast carriage used ashore
chines	the end of a cask holding the staves together
clipper	fast nineteenth-century sailing ship with fine lines
cockpit	after part of the orlop deck, in action devoted to the care of the wounded
colours	the national ensign of the navy or port of registry of the ship

convoy	an effective method of gathering together individual ships under the protection of an armed escort
corsair	originally those on both sides engaged in the Mediterranean wars between Christian and Moor, later applied to armed predators that are not warships
cupola	rounded covering atop a tower
cutting out	a daring raid in boats to cut the cables of an enemy ship and bring it out
double	at sea, to achieve the rounding of a prominence; to double a cape
double-banked	equipped with extra guns on the spar deck, or in a boat two men on each oar
dovetail	method of interlocking joints in wood or stone
driver	large fore and aft sail rigged abaft the mizzenmast to counterbalance the sails going from the foremast to the bowsprit
firebrand	crude flaming torch for illumination
fireship	expendable vessel filled with combustibles, set afire and sent into an enemy anchorage
first-rate	a man of war with 100 or more guns
flagship	a ship flying the flag of a rear admiral or above
forecastle	the section of the upper deck furthest forward; pronounced 'fokesel'
foreyard	lowest and largest yard on the foremast
foul	various nautical meanings, generally something at cross purposes
founder	when a ship sinks completely beneath the waves as opposed to wrecking on the rocks
frigate	full-rigged ship with one deck of guns
full dress uniform	formal uniform, with gold lace and ceremonial sword
galleon	fifteenth- through seventeenth-century ship used both as a warship and a trader
gang cask	small, portable keg
general chase	the order to attack the enemy as independent ships, not in a line of battle
gibbet	metal cage to display corpses of executed criminals
grapeshot	iron balls bound together in a bag, which scatter like shotgun pellets when fired from a cannon
grog	usually rum, the daily ration issued to the sailors mixed with water; from Admiral Vernon, 'Old Grogram', after his cloak
guardship	warship set on station at a port
gun money, head money	to compensate seamen for taking on a tough man-of-war instead of a fat merchant ship, based on the number of opposing guns and men
hawse	that part of the ship where the anchor cable leaves the vessel and goes into the water; disturbing operations here while working ship would be resented
heel	to deliberately incline a ship to one side
hemp	fibre of the cannabis family used for high-quality rope
hogshead	capacity varied, but up to 60 gallons

in reserve	a ship not needed for immediate use, taken down to the bare bones
inns of court	London-based association of English lawyers
keel	the spine of a ship lying at the lowest point of the frames
knot	in speed, one nautical mile per hour
larboard	the old word for port, the left-hand side of the ship as seen when facing the bow
leat	channel cut to extract and lead water away from a river
lee shore	a shore downwind of the ship where she can be blown to destruction
light dragoons	horse soldier who can also serve on foot
log line	the line attached to the log that measures a ship's speed through the water
main chains	hardware used to secure the lower shrouds of the mainmast outside the ship's side
maltster	prepares malt used in brewing beer
man-of-war	warship as opposed to a merchantman
marline spike	an iron spike used for separating strands of rope before splicing
master	in the navy this is a warrant officer responsible for navigation and sailing of a warship for the captain; in the merchant service it is the captain of a ship
master-at-arms	responsible for police duties and small-arms training aboard a naval ship
midshipman	apprentice officer in the navy
mizzen	the aftermost mast of three in a ship
mortar	a short cannon for throwing heavy shells in a parabola
oakum	teased out old rope used for caulking deck seams
orlop	lowest deck in a ship of the line, directly over the hold
packet	mail-boat regularly plying between two ports, also carrying passengers and goods
painter	rope fixed to a boat's bow for holding it secure
phantom arm	the sensation that an amputated arm feels still attached to the body
pike	a defensive lance used against boarders
pilot	seaman with expert local knowledge hired to see a vessel safely into port
pipe	a barrel, quantity varies, but around 100 gallons; (2) boatswain's order using his whistle
post captain	captain of a post ship, an important man-of-war with more than 20 guns
powder hulk	immobilised vessel used to store ammunition
privateer	an armed merchant vessel holding a licence (letter of marque) from its national government to attack enemy trade
prize crew	that part of the ship's company detailed to take charge of a captured ship and sail her to the nearest home port
quarterdeck	the upper deck past the mainmast; that part of the ship from which the captain and officers take command

quarters	battle stations
reef	reduce sail area by tying off a section
rigger	dockyardman skilled in setting up a ship's rigging
rigging	standing rigging are ropes holding masts steady; running rigging are the lines operating the sails
roadstead	area outside a harbour suitable as a mass anchorage
rocket	missile self-propelled with gunpowder
rope-walk	long passageway where strands of yarn are twisted together to make rope
royal yard men	very skilled sailors who work aloft on the highest sails of all
royalist	Frenchman still loyal to King Louis
schooner	vessel with two masts, the higher one aft, and the sails fore and aft, rather than square across
scimitar	the characteristic curved sword of a Moor
sea room	plenty of sea space for a square-rigged ship to perform daring manoeuvres
sheet anchor	backup anchor if the main one fails
ship of the line	a ship capable of taking her place in the line of battle during a major action
shrouds	stout ropes supporting either side of a mast, fitted with climbing lines
sloop of war	vessel captained by a commander, who is junior to a full captain
small beer	beer with an inferior alcoholic content, used instead of water aboard ship
spar	general name for mast or yard
spar deck	semi-enclosed deck above the main-deck
stern gallery	balcony built outside the body of the ship at the stern
strake	horizontal strip of wooden planking of the hull
strike	lower, put out of action; used for sails or the colours
supernumerary	someone in addition to the established ship's complement
sweeps	long heavy oars used in a small ship
tender	a vessel that attends a man-of-war, primarily in harbour, bringing supplies, men, etc.
Texel	an important Dutch anchorage off the coast of the Netherlands
tobacco stopper	for tamping down the fire of a clay pipe
tops	the place where a topmast is fitted into the lower mast. A fighting platform was often added for sharpshooters
tricolore	French Revolutionary flag
under weigh	the point in the process of hoisting the anchor when it is clear of the seabed – under way is when the vessel starts moving through the water
warrant officer	an officer below commissioned rank, holding a warrant from the Admiralty
weight of metal	the total weight of one cannonball from each of the guns in a broadside; a measure of firepower
yardarm	either of the ends of a yard

Index

Picture Acknowledgements

The following images are in the public domain:-

page 81 from Charles Darwin, *A Naturalist's Voyage Around the World*, 1913, illustration by R.T. Pritchett

page 82 mezzo-tint of 1768 by P. L. Tassaert, after an oil painting by Thomas King, 1767

page 88 'A Scene Between Decks' by W. J. Huggins in Charles N Robinson, *The British Tar in Fact and Fiction,* 1909

page 92 'The Sailor's Description of a Chase and Capture', coloured etching by George Cruikshank

page 94 'Mastheaded' by J. E. Edwards in Charles N Robinson, *The British Tar in Fact and Fiction,* 1909

page 95 'Victors of the Nile', a celebratory engraving published five years after the Battle of the Nile

page 96 'A Sailor', R. Cruikshank, 1827

page 98 early nineteenth-century engraving by Thomas Rowlandson

page 100 from Peter Cordingley, *The Maritime Compendium*

page 102 'Colours Warranted Not to Run' from Charles N Robinson, *The British Tar in Fact and Fiction,* 1909

page 103 'The Armada Portrait', one of three surviving versions of an allegorical panel painting. Artist: George Gower, c 1588.

page 105 image by nineteenth-century French painter Antoine Morel-Fatio

page 106 'A Greenwich Pensioner' by R Cruikshank from Charles N Robinson, *The British Tar in Fact and Fiction,* 1909

page 107 engraving by John Chapman, 1797

page 112 from Charles N Robinson, *The British Tar in Fact and Fiction,* 1909

page 116 'On the Look-Out!' from Charles N. Robinson, *The British Fleet,* 1894

page 117 from D. and J.T. Serres, *Liber Nauticus,* 1805

page 119 'A Ship's Cook' by Thomas Rowlandson c. 1799

page 121 contemporary mezzo-tint

page 123 from Jones, *Views of the Seats of Noblemen and Gentlemen,* 1829

page 128 from Olaus Magnus, *Historia de Gentibus Septentrionalibus* (History of the Northern Peoples) 1555

page 129 title page, *Sir Francis Drake Revived,* 1626.

page 130 'Neptune, King of Waters', engraving by Virgil Solis for Ovid's *Metamorphoses*

page 132 caricature of a press gang, 1780

page 133 from Dante's *Inferno* , illustration by Gustave Doré

page 135 print by J. J. Baugean from *Receuil de Petites Marines,* 1819

page 138 illustration by Birket Foster, engraving by William Miller, 1872

page 140 image traditionally believed to represent Antonio Pigafetta, artist unknown

page 143 'The Battle of Trafalgar' by William Clarkson Stanfield, engraving by William Miller, 1839

page 146 advertisement from 'The Ladies' World', March 1898

page 148 from G. Hartwig, *The Aerial World,* 1886

page 149 Olaus Magnus, *Historia de gentibus septentrionalibus,* 1555

page 151 'Illustrated London News' October 28, 1848

page 152 Bibliothèque Nationale

page 158 engraving by William Miller, 1875, after J M W Turner

page 160 from John Masefield, *On the Spanish Main*

page 162 'The Ghosts of Admiral Hosier and His Men Appearing to Admiral Vernon', coloured etching published in July 1740 by C. Mosley
page 164 coloured aqua-tint by J. T. Lee, engraved by Robert Dodd, March 1804
page 166 engraving from a portrait by Sir George Chambers
page 167 nineteenth-century illustration by William Bradford
page 168 from Peter Cordingley, *The Maritime Compendium*
page 170 eighteenth-century illustration
page 174 from Stanley Lane-Poole, *The Story of the Barbary Corsairs*, published 1890
page 176 illustration by Henry Winstanley, 1696
page 179 image over 100 years old, no details available
page 180 map from the July 1750 issue of 'The Gentleman's Magazine'; attributed to Moses Harris, a naturalist and surveyor.
page 181 eighteenth-century drawing
page 185 black and white image of the wreck of *Loch Leven*, still under full sail, from 'Illustrated Sydney News', 25 November 1871, artist unknown
page 187 painting by Arnald George (1763–1841)

The following individuals/organisations have kindly given permission to use images:-

page 24 Jeremy Johns
page 33 The Marine Society & Sea Cadets
page 76 courtesy of the U.S. Navy
page 90 Annette M. Onslow

Author Acknowledgements

My sincere appreciation to all at Ebury Press, especially Carey Smith and Vicky Orchard for their editorial vision and guidance. Thanks, too, are due to David Fordham for his splendid book design. And I cannot omit my gratitude to two other very wonderful women, my agent Carole Blake for her enthusiasm for the project, and my wife Kathy for her assistance at every level.